TRUMPED-UP CHARGES!

Donald Trump Didn't Say Mexicans are Rapists and Criminals, and 9 Other Lies about Him Exposed

By Constantinos E. Scaros

Foreword by U.S. Congressman Gus Bilirakis

Copyright © 2020 by Constantinos E. Scaros
Front and Back Cover Photos
(Shutterstock Enhanced License)

To the canons of journalism, and to all who have the courage to proclaim: "I think I'm right, but I could be wrong."

ABOUT THE AUTHOR

Constantinos E. Scaros BA, MA, JD, PhD – is a presidential historian, educator, attorney, newspaper editor and columnist, and political analyst. He is the author of several books, including *Stop Calling Them "Immigrants"* – which is available in print and e-book

TABLE OF CONTENTS

FOREWORD – by U.S. Congressman Gus Bilirakis	7
PREFACE – Why I Wrote This Book	11
INTRODUCTION – Fake News: Why They Lie about Donald Trump	15
CHAPTER 1 – Trump Didn't Say "Mexicans are Rapists and Criminals"	29
CHAPTER 2 – Trump Didn't Mock a Reporter's Physical Disability	39
CHAPTER 3 – Trump Didn't Call Carly Fiorina Ugly	51
CHAPTER 4 – Trump Didn't Refuse to Disavow David Duke	63
CHAPTER 5 – Trump Didn't Call White Supremacists "Very Fine People"	79
HALFTIME REMINDER	91
CHAPTER 6 – Trump Didn't Brag about Committing Sexual Assault	93
CHAPTER 7 – Trump Didn't Issue a Muslim Ban	107
CHAPTER 8 – Trump Didn't Make up Hurricane Dorian's Risk of Striking Alabama	119
CHAPTER 9 – Trump Does Not Encourage Violence at His Rallies or Elsewhere	129
continued on next page	

TABLE OF CONTENTS (continued)

CHAPTER 10 – Trump Didn't Say Four Congresswomen Should "Go Back to Their Countries"	149
CONCLUSION – What This Book Proves	161
AFTERWORD – Is Trump a Racist? Speculation vs. Analysis	165
EPILOGUE – After the Impeachment	167
ACKNOWLEDGMENTS	171

FOREWORD
By U.S. Congressman Gus Bilirakis

It's been a handful of years since I met Constantinos Scaros, a guy who shares my name, but uses the more urbane version – Dino – of Constantine than the "Gus" I was born with.

I immediately bonded with Dino. He is smart, funny, and, like me, loves the Greek culture but is first and foremost an American. And he's is easy to talk to. So, suffice it to say, that I was thrilled to meet Dr. Scaros.

As a member of Congress who serves on two very important committees (Energy and Commerce, and Veterans Affairs), I am very busy attending hearings, briefings, meetings; participate in events and delivering speeches; and, reviewing legislation and digesting any number of memoranda on upcoming votes.

Somewhere among all of that, I try to spend a little time with my wife and four boys. Free time to indulge in a great book is limited. That's why when I do grab something to read, I want it to be as informative and concise as possible with enough pizzazz to keep me engaged.

Enter the brilliant Dino Scaros. Here's a guy who writes like he talks. I can understand him. He is not highfalutin. Though a college professor, Dr. Scaros is not a stuffy academic preaching from some ivory tower. He is just a guy who wants us to think differently. Think analytically. Really just use common sense. Like me, he is not blindly partisan. He just wants government to function properly, honestly. I pride myself in being bipartisan. Recently, Vanderbilt University noted in a study of all 535 members of Congress and the U.S. Senate, that I was one of the most effective legislators overall, and the most effective in the Florida delegation. That means my colleagues, both Republican and Democrat, trust me. It's not in me to be a political bomb thrower and take pot shots for the evening news soundbites. I'm not prone to hyperbole. Neither is Dino. He tells it like it is. That's why I like reading and digesting his stuff. I know he's not going to hoodwink me like some slick-talking colleagues I work with.

Dino Scaros has a knack for understanding what people want. This was proved in his great book *Grumpy Old Party*. It was as though he had a sixth sense. He knew in 2015 that voters had finally had it with the political establishments. They were longing for something different. So, Dino wrote a playbook essentially that would revolutionize the Republican Party. Essential guidelines that called for a maverick like Donald J. Trump to pick up and run with. And, run he did.

Dino was so prescient with his counsel, that now I turn to him on all matters of politics. His advice, against all odds, helped get Donald Trump elected. I have no doubt this latest book will help get the president reelected. The painstaking research and thoughtful analysis put into *Trumped-Up Charges!* absolutely elucidates how scandalous the mainstream media is. I don't say that lightly, either. I have always believed the media should be the watchdog of government. A free and fair press distinguishes our great nation from all others. Unlike other nations, government corruption is not institutionalized in the United States because our press is free and relentless. It can and must root out government officials acting in bad faith. But, when the media is so biased that it renders itself not believable by the electorate, then we are in big trouble. Once the media is ignored, it becomes irrelevant. When it becomes irrelevant, who will be the watchdog of government? It's a serious problem to be solved in another book.

But here, *Trumped-Up Charges!* shows us with painstaking detail why and how President Trump and his supporters have so much animus towards the media. This is a book every First Amendment-loving person should read. I plan on sharing it with my Democratic colleagues in Congress as well as the handful of "Never-Trump" Republicans who still can't abide the fact that we finally have a president who has fulfilled his campaign promises.

Neither I, nor Dino, if I may be presumptuous, are Trump apologists. We're just fans of fairness. And, if my friends are being intellectually honest with themselves, they'll share this book with their liberal friends in the media and tell them to stop the madness!

Kudos to Dino Scaros for shining the light on the media and its malfeasance. You will recognize immediately each of the ten instances of gross media bias outlined in *Trumped-Up Charges!* And, I'm sure like me, you cringed initially when Donald Trump made some of the comments noted in the text. But, this book will show how wrong you were (I was) to buy into the media's false narrative. Hopefully, this will encourage the journalists to make themselves relevant again by putting aside the bias and getting back to Reporting 101.

I appreciate Dino Scaros' commitment to fairness and accuracy. With *Trumped-Up Charges!* he has become the watchdog of the media. And, we should all be grateful for his efforts.

Gus Bilirakis - 12th Congressional District – FL
U.S. House of Representatives
March, 2020

PREFACE
Why I Wrote This Book

Do you or someone you know really dislike Donald Trump? Do you wish he wasn't president any longer? Do you hope he loses reelection or better yet, is thrown out of office sooner than that? Why do you feel this way?

What if you found out that Trump really didn't say that "Mexicans are rapists and criminals," that he really didn't make fun of a reporter's physical disability, that he really didn't impose a ban on Muslims, and that he really didn't call white supremacists "very fine people"? What if you were to learn that those and many other stories about him were false? Would that change your view of him? And even if it didn't, wouldn't you still prefer to know the truth? Don't you – and all Americans – deserve to know the truth?"

I have had many jobs over the years. As I write this, I continue to be a teacher, a historian, and a political analyst and columnist. My newspaper columns are opinionated, as they are supposed to be; but when I teach history, government, and political science – whether to fifth graders or college seniors – and when I write about history, I remain as evenhanded as possible. The same holds true whenever I write a news story – such as when I covered Donald Trump's Republican presidential primary victory in New York on April 19, 2016. Live from Trump Tower, I described that Tuesday evening's events, which all but guaranteed Trump would win the party's nomination. Although I was very happy about it, I didn't let it show in my article – or in subsequent lectures I delivered in academic settings. And if I were to write about it in a history book, I wouldn't tip my hand about my political preferences in that forum either.

History is supposed to be an account of the truth, a gatekeeper of accuracy. It ought to present as complete a picture as possible so that future generations, not even born at the time the events in question took place, can absorb the pure, unfiltered data and draw their own conclusions – just as we would expect a true account of the weather in Los Angeles, CA on January 15, 1967, the place and date on which the Green Bay Packers and the Kansas City Chiefs competed in the first ever Super Bowl.

Ever since Trump's famous escalator arrival on June 16, 2015 to a Trump Tower press conference announcing his presidential candidacy in the following year's election, he has fallen victim to a relentless barrage of misinformation. The motives for these falsehoods are less important than the consequences: tens of millions of Americans continue to believe bad things about President Trump that simply aren't true.

After reading this book, in which 10 of the most-told lies and out-of-context half-truths about Trump are exposed, many readers who criticized Trump in the past will change their minds about him – but others won't. Even in the election of 1984, in which President Reagan captured an astounding 49 out of 50 states as well as Washington, DC, he only won about 59% of the vote; over 38 million Americans voted for someone else.[1] Similarly, Donald Trump will never convince 100 percent of the population to support him; no politician will. Elections boil down to priorities and faith: 1) the issues most important to a particular voter; and 2) the candidate the voter believes is best-equipped to handle those issues effectively.

The main reason I wrote this book is to set the record straight. Whether Americans ultimately stand with Donald Trump or stand against him, they deserve to know the truth about him. That will place them in the best position from which to draw an informed and educated conclusion.

INTRODUCTION
Fake News: Why They Lie about Donald Trump

I am a presidential historian. I've been studying the presidents ever since I was a kid. In college, I majored in political science and double minored in journalism and history. I hold a master's degree and a PhD in history. Both my master's thesis and my doctoral dissertation are about the American presidency. This is what I do. As I write this, less than a year before the 2020 election, I consider myself a very strong Trump supporter in the sense that it is hard for me to imagine any potentially viable candidate better-suited to be president at this time.

As recently as mid-June 2015, though, even after that historic escalator ride and announcement that he was running for president, I was far from being a Trump fan. Oh, I had nothing against him, it's just that he was irrelevant to me. And it was nothing personal. In all of our busy lives, we only have a certain amount of available time, and a universe of people, places, or things on which to focus. And so, we have to choose. For me, choosing to be interested in or to learn more about successful businesspersons – whether Donald Trump, Bill Gates, or Warren Buffett – simply wasn't for me.

I've always said "good for them," just like I'd say "good for them" about various Olympians – from downhill ski racers to figure skaters to javelin throwers – but that isn't for me either (give me the NFL or the NBA any day). I am also not a reality show watcher. To this day, I haven't watched a single episode of *The Apprentice* – whether hosted by Trump or anyone else – and have no idea on what channel it appeared. I didn't find it "juicy" that Trump was married and divorced, and married again and again, nor did I ever care about the size of the ring he gave his fiancées/wives. My only reference to Trump in an occasional conversation would be to equate him to a rich person. For instance, I still remember that while vacationing on one particularly primitive Greek island in the late 1980s, I remarked at how amazingly inexpensive everything was (mixed drinks, for example, cost about the equivalent of 35 cents apiece!) by saying: "there's nothing Donald Trump can do on this island that I can't."

All that changed, for a short while, in the year 2000. I spent some of that summer on the beaches of Eastern Long Island (NY) reading his then-recently published book, *The America We Deserve*.[2] It was a book on how to fix the United States, from domestic matters to foreign affairs. It was a prototype of "Make America Great Again." At that moment, Trump was no longer a dealmaking real estate tycoon. He was an aspiring presidential candidate, and so my ears perked up.

Trump's flirtation with presidential politics faded away, though, as third party nominees included Pat Buchanan and Ralph Nader, and the election centered on Republican George W. Bush, who defeated Democrat Al Gore by the narrowest of Electoral College margins, setting in motion a recount controversy ultimately settled by the U.S. Supreme Court legally, even as it did not provide universal closure.[3] As Trump stepped back from a White House run, I reverted to thinking of him as "generic rich guy," for whom I had no particular positive or negative opinions.

Again, all of that changed in the summer of 2015. When Trump announced his candidacy in June, my family and I were out of the country; I was on a working vacation – among other things, I was completing the first draft of my book *Grumpy Old Party*, about what was wrong with the Republican Party and what it needed to do to win back the White House.[4] At the time, I had absolutely no idea that Trump would even enter the race, let alone win. My wife suggested that I enjoy my vacation and not spend so much time poring over the news, so I tried to confine myself to reading only the headlines as much as possible. "Trump calls

Mexicans 'Rapists' and 'Criminals'" was the first headline I came across on June 16 when I logged on to my laptop, and I fell for the clickbait. "This thing is turning into a circus," I said aloud, to my wife, who was in the next room. "Now Donald Trump just entered the race. Can you believe it? And he started off by saying Mexicans are rapists and criminals."

(NOTE: On first impression, one might consider the phrase "rapists and criminals" to be awkward, since a rapist is a type of criminal, and therefore to say "rapists and criminals" would imply that a rapist is not a criminal. The phrasing itself is irrelevant, other than to point out that Trump never actually uttered the three-word phrase "rapists and criminals"; the media who is out to get him did that. Later versions changed the phrase to "rapists and thugs," though Trump never used the word "thugs" in that speech, though he has used it on other occasions to describe gang members.)

Within a few weeks, we were back home, and spent the night at my cousins' house in New York. While sitting on their front porch having a drink late that evening, my one cousin and I began talking about the 2016 race, and he said, to my surprise: "I love Donald Trump!" My response – and in retrospect I feel so foolish to have taken that headline clickbait – was: "Really? I can't take him seriously. I can't get over what he said about Mexico – he basically trashed an entire country. He said 'Mexicans are rapists and criminals.'" My cousin replied: "That's not what he said. He actually said 'Mexico *is sending* rapists and criminals.' Look at the video, you'll see." The jetlag was setting in, and my brain needed a break. Later that week, while in my own home and with the jetlag gone, I examined the issue in greater detail and realized my cousin was right. We'll discuss the details in Chapter 1, but for now, consider that I was thoroughly disgusted: not at Trump, but at the media's treatment of him. I began staunchly defending him, not for the sake of promoting his candidacy, but because I wanted to promote the truth and expose the media's lies.

Eventually, I did become a "born-again Trumpie." That was in early August, after watching the first Republican primary debate. At that moment, I realized not only that Trump had an excellent chance of winning the nomination and the general election – "a giant among dwarfs" I wrote at the time – but I also began to appreciate and support his candidacy, and I've never looked back.

My enthusiasm for Trump is only incidental to the main purpose of this book, and in some ways detrimental to it. Admittedly, my argument would be even more compelling if I was not a Trump fan. As it stands, some naysayers might dismiss my arguments as self-serving. Yet my quest to exonerate Trump from false charges began *before* I became a fan. My goal was to expose what the mainstream media had become, not to boost Trump's chances of winning.

Before we delve into the various lies and out-of-context half-truths the media has spewed about Trump at least since June, 2015, thereby betraying their obligations as journalists, let's examine why the media distorts the truth so callously and routinely in the first place. To say "they hate Trump" is an oversimplification, because Trump is not their only victim. Nonetheless, there is no doubt that there is some personal animosity in place, partly because unlike most other presidents who brush off cheap shots by the press, Trump highlights them and hits back twice as hard. Many reporters, not used to being hit back, clearly can dish it out but can't take it.

Another reason much of the media seems to be obsessed with bringing down President Trump is ideological. It is no secret that the overwhelming majority of the media leans left. For example, in 2014 Trump had yet to enter the presidential race, but in extensive interviews with over a thousand journalists that year, only 7 percent of them self-identified as Republican.[5] In October, 2016, just weeks before the election, the Center for Public Integrity revealed that of journalists who made campaign contributions to Trump or to his main opponent, Democrat Hillary Clinton, an overwhelming 96 percent of the donations were for Clinton.[6] Granted, some of that bias may have been personal (in favor of Clinton and/or against Trump), but political and ideological leanings surely must factor heavily in such an astonishingly lopsided statistic. Besides, many in the media not so long ago had blasted other prominent Republicans who were neither abrasive nor confrontational in return – President George W. Bush most readily comes to mind. Nonetheless, there has been a drastic change over the past couple of decades in how journalists report the news. In his 2003 book *Journalistic Fraud: How the New York Times Distorts the News and Why it Can No Longer Be Trusted*, Bob Kohn made a strong case – providing many examples – of why the *Times*, long considered the "newspaper of record," had tarnished its good name by injecting opinion into its news stories.[7]

Beyond ideology, the media is interested in personal survival. For newspapers and newscasts to continue to exist, they must be relevant. They must have readerships and audiences. Eric

Alterman wrote in *The Nation* that "our independent media is under attack" because the administration "and its ideological allies are employing every means available to undermine journalists' ability to exercise their First Amendment function to hold power accountable," and the administration "recognizes no such constitutional role for the press."[8] The administration to which Alterman referred, though, was that of the younger President Bush. In fact, the *Times* in particular seemed to take the most exception to Bush's comment – not calling the media "fake news," as Trump does, but rather flippantly declaring in 2003 that "I don't read newspapers."[9] In fact, in a Christmas day article three years later, the *Times* continued to obsess about the president's snub, providing contradictory information and concluding that Bush did read newspapers after all.[10]

The *Times* was a fixture in my house ever since I could remember. My dad read it from cover to cover every day. He was interested in the writing quality, not necessarily the political leanings. He encouraged me to read it every day so that I would write well too. I attempted to read it every now and then when I was nine or ten years old, but the writing was a tad too sophisticated for me; I preferred the other local New York papers, the *Post* and the *Daily News*. They were easier to read: they had comics and better sports sections. By the sixth grade, though, our entire class was given a subscription to the *Times*, and from that point on until 30 years later, in 2006, I read it every day.

My "divorce after a 30-year marriage" from the *Times*, as I described it then, was based on my realization of its eroding standards of journalism. Too many of my colleagues reflexively continued to refer to it as "the paper of record" and "the finest newspaper in the world," and I challenged them to take a more careful look because, no pun intended, times had changed. I remember many instances of that erosion during 2006 and thought to myself: "I can't take it anymore," but changing from my go-to newspaper after 30 years was easier said than done. Finally, the last straw was on December 7. The day before, a bipartisan study group delivered its recommendations to Congress about changing the focus and strategy regarding the Iraq War. The straightforward report was long on analysis and admirably devoid of partisan bickering. There was hardly any indication that the panel had put the blame on President Bush. Having read the report online, I predicted that somehow, the *Times* would spin the following morning's headline to read: "In a Blow to Bush, Iraq Study Group Calls for Major Changes."[11] The actual headline was: "Panel Urges Basic Shift in U.S. Policy in Iraq," with the subheadline "Rebuke for Bush – Situation is 'Grave.'"[12] That was close enough; my 30-year relationship with the *Times* had come to an end.

Ten years later, Trump escalated the awareness of media bias, but he really got under the press' skin when he took to social media, particularly Twitter. By communicating directly with the American people via tweets, Trump cut out the middleman – the establishment media. Add to that Trump's disdain for establishmentarian politics and Capitol Hill institutions and it is no wonder why the *Washington Post* – the ultimate Beltway insider – took the lead in condemning his candidacy. In its editorial – the title is self-explanatory – "Hillary Clinton for President," the *Post* described Trump as "bigoted, ignorant, deceitful, narcissistic, vengeful, petty, misogynistic, fiscally reckless, intellectually lazy, contemptuous of democracy and enamored of America's enemies. As president, he would pose a grave danger to the nation and the world."[13] Clearly, the "grave danger" the *Post* had realized a Trump presidency would pose would be to its own relevance; in the media business the one thing more unbearable than being hated is being ignored. The *Boston Globe*, owned by the New York Times Company and considered one of the more long-respected broadsheet newspapers in the United States, in a maneuver completely out of character, published a satirical front page in its April 10, 2016 edition – seven months before that year's election – about what the United States under a Trump administration might look like."[14] Some of the headlines, captions and quotes, with a dateline a year into the future (April 9, 2017), read: "Curfews Extended in Multiple Cities"…"Dow Declines at Record Pace"…"U.S. Soldiers Refuse to Kill ISIS Families"…and "New Law Targets 'Absolute Scum' in the Press."[15]

Also extremely surprising is that the majority of newspapers throughout the United States that typically endorse Republican candidates either endorsed Clinton, another non-Trump candidate, or no one at all in the 2016 presidential election. "Damn Right, We're with Her," the New York *Daily News* titled its Clinton-endorsing editorial.[16] The *Houston Chronicle* explained that were it virtually any other Republican running against Clinton, they would have considered their choice more carefully, but in the case of Trump, he is a "danger to the republic."[17] The *Arizona Republic*'s editorial is in some ways the most telling about why typically Republican-leaning newspapers rejected Trump: "he is not conservative."[18] The newspaper then rambled on about Trump being unfit to be president, citing as fact some of the accusations this book proves to be false, but it showed its true colors with the "not a conservative" remark. On that note, they weren't wrong: Trump never claimed to be a staunch conservative. He famously called for a one-time 14.5% wealth tax on individuals and trusts with a net worth over $10 million in *The America We Deserve*, and challenged the doctrine of trickle-down economics, particularly early on in the 2016 campaign.[19]

Trump also said that although he believes in God, "I don't like to bother Him with prayer" which is an anathema to so many Evangelical Christians, for whom prayer is not just a means to an end but a way of life in itself. He threatened to place tariffs on foreign goods of countries that abused trade privileges (and he made good on that threat as president), which made Wall Streeters cringe, and his stance against illegal entry and stay – arguably the strongest by any president in 100 years – not only is alarming to the left, which wants to import (future Democratic) votes and redo the Western European-dominated American culture, but also to those on the right who turn the other way at PHI (Persons Here Illegally) workers, because cheap labor helps the economy's overall bottom line. All three of those newspapers endorsed Republican Mitt Romney in 2012; the *Republic*, in fact, boasted that it had never endorsed a Democrat since its inception in 1890.[20]

Ideology – both the left and the right are opposed to Trumpism (which differs from Republicanism and traditional conservatism) – is one of the two main reasons most of the media turned on Trump ever since he announced his candidacy, and haven't stopped. The other big reason, tied to the aforementioned aspect of survival, is ratings. A study over several decades conducted by Gallup shows how Americans increasingly turn away from newspapers and television for their news, relying on social media and their smartphones in particular, instead.[21] For example, over 50 percent of poll respondents indicated that in 1998 they read their local newspapers daily, compared to just 19 percent in 2019.[22] In 1995, 62 percent watched the news on one of "the big three" network stations – ABC, CBS, and NBC – every evening, compared to 27 percent in 2019.[23] By comparison, a mere 3 percent received their news from an electronic gadget – such as a computer or phone – in 1995, as compared to a whopping 49 percent in 2019.[24] By turning on Trump for calling them Fake News, the mainstream media simultaneously hit back at their top enemy and sensationalize their reporting so as to compete with the brasher and more colorful social media outlets, such as Facebook and Twitter.

Now that we've explained why the media distorts the truth about Donald Trump, let's take a look at 10 key examples of when they have done so.

CHAPTER 1
Trump Didn't Say
"Mexicans are Rapists and Criminals"

On June 16, 2015, Donald Trump launched his 2016 presidential bid with a press conference from his New York City landmark headquarters, Trump Tower. He literally had not even finished speaking when the false message that he had called Mexicans "rapists" and "criminals" spread like wildfire.

The one-sentence clickbait headlines on various webpages set the tone, and soon enough millions of Americans believed that Trump had called an entire nation of people rapists and criminals. Some had no problem with that. But many more, including me, found it shameful to denigrate an entire nation of people. As I explained in the Introduction, I fell for the clickbait trap; unlike millions of other Americans, though, I soon recognized the error of my ways and became even more committed to finding the truth and exposing lies.

What I continue to find fascinating is that even to this day, so many people with whom I discuss this topic insist: "but he *did* call them 'rapists' and 'criminals,'" going so far as to say: "I heard him say it. On the news. Look it up. You can find the video on the Internet. It's there." On a couple of occasions, I looked up the video on the spot and showed them to prove my point.

Here is the exact language Trump used on that mid-June day: "When Mexico sends its people, they're not sending their best. They're not sending you. They're not sending you. They're sending people that have lots of problems, and they're bringing those problems with us. They're bringing drugs. They're bringing crime. They're rapists. And some, I assume, are good people. But I speak to border guards and they tell us what we're getting. And it only makes common sense. It only makes common sense. They're sending us not the right people."[25]

Let's start with *the first three* words: "When Mexico sends..." Everything that follows describes the people Mexico sends, not all Mexicans who live in Mexico, and certainly not all Mexicans throughout the world. By "Mexico," Trump doesn't mean the country itself, because a country is an inanimate object that cannot engage in the activity of sending anyone anywhere. Trump confirms this by then substituting the word "they're" for "Mexico" in his subsequent words: "they're not sending their best. They're not sending you. They're not sending you." These "they," therefore, are people from Mexico. They could be criminals, such as druglords, gunrunners, and human traffickers.

Naturally, it would make sense that hardened criminals interested in furthering their criminal enterprise to other countries would send "bad" people, not law-abiding folks. I cannot imagine anyone would have a problem that Trump may have offended "people senders" from Mexico who are criminals.

Suppose instead that the senders in question were not hardened criminals? Who else could they be? Certainly not law-abiding Mexican citizens. By definition, those who keep on the straight and narrow surely wouldn't send "rapists" and "criminals" to another country, would they? The only suspect left is the Mexican government itself. Would "they" – meaning the government – want to rid its country of its bad apples by encouraging them to get out of Mexico and move to the United States, and even assisting them to do so. From a selfish perspective, it would make a great deal of sense: get rid of the bad people and keep the good people. What government wouldn't want a country full of good people? Obviously, though, such behavior by any government would be highly inappropriate. Only a corrupt government would do such a thing.

At worst, it seems that Trump may have overstepped his criticism, accusing the Mexican government of doing something terrible. If his charges were unfounded, then Mexico's elected officials at the time would have every right to be offended, as would the citizens of Mexico insofar as Trump would have insulted their government.

Nonetheless, none of that in any way suggests that Trump made a blanket generalization that Mexicans as a whole are rapists and criminals. It is not as if Trump said: "hey, look, here comes Carlos walking down the street. He's Mexican, so he must be a rapist and a criminal."

Also, there is no certainty that Trump meant that the "rapists" and "criminals" in question are even Mexican. Since the election, he has highlighted the problem of caravans traveling through Central America through Mexico headed for the United States.[26] Analogously, Syrian refugees have poured onto the Greek islands in droves over the past few years, in hopes of ultimately settling in more prosperous Western European countries. If a French, German, or Italian politician were to say "Greece is sending 'rapists' and 'criminals,'" whether or not there was any merit either to the Greek government's complicity in "sending" or if any of the Syrian refugees in question were criminals, could anyone really plausibly argue that the politician in question "called Greeks 'rapists' and 'criminals'"? Granted, when Trump used the words "its people" to describe who "Mexico is sending," it would imply that they are Mexicans. But a few seconds later in that same speech, Trump said "it's coming from more than Mexico. It's coming from all over South and Latin America, and it's coming probably – probably – from the Middle East."[27] In his own words, Trump defined the problem as coming from various regions of the world, diverse in nationality and culture, yet the media spin was that he singled out Mexicans as his target. While I am not in the habit of overspeculating, it doesn't take much to figure how such a narrative could have a very negative impact on Trump regarding support from the large voting bloc of Latino-Americans.

Assuming for the moment that Trump accused the Mexican government of sending the worst people in their country over the border, a more appropriate headline might have been: "Trump implies Mexican government is sending 'Rapists' and 'Criminals' to the United States." In that case, critics might accuse him of being paranoid and touting delusional conspiracy theories. Even if that were the case, that is much different than accusing him of degrading an entire nationality. In any case, before we leave this chapter it is important not only to address the original accusation – which clearly has been debunked – but also the related point that if Trump accused the Mexican government of being corrupt, there was merit to the claim and it was not some outlandish speculation created out of thin air.

First, taking someone at his word – in this case, Donald Trump, though to some that simply defies the bounds of acceptability – is a logical first step: where is Trump getting the information that there are rapists and criminals coming across the Southern border to begin with? According to him, from Border Patrol Agents. Not coincidentally, the National Border Patrol Council (NBPC), which is the official national organization representing border patrol agents, in 2016 for the first time ever endorsed a candidate, Trump, in a presidential primary, proclaiming that they would not "shy away from voicing our opinions as it pertains to border security and the men and women of the United States Border Patrol. We think it is that important: if we do not secure our borders, American communities will continue to suffer at the hands of gangs, cartels and violent criminals preying on the innocent. The lives and security of the American people are at stake, and the National Border Patrol Council will not sit on the sidelines."[28]

Was the Mexican government really so corrupt that it would intentionally gather up its criminals and ship them off to the United States? Absent an actual thorough and unbiased investigation, it seems the answer will continue to be based on speculation rather than fact. Nonetheless, there are two pieces of information that are useful, not so much in confirming that implication but in establishing that the notion is by no means outrageous. First, there is the annual report issued by Transparency International, the leading global nonprofit committed to fighting government corruption in all countries throughout the world: in 2015, it ranked 168 countries and territories on a scale of 0 (highly corrupt) to 100 (very clean), and Mexico scored a mere 31, tying with Honduras, Mauritania, Malawe, Mozambique, and Vietnam for 111th on the list, well below the international average.[29] In fact, Mexico's already low 2014 score of 35 dropped four points in 2015, the year in which Trump made the remarks.

Next, there is article published in the *New York Times* – which is certainly no fan of Trump – reporting that the Mexican government published a pamphlet instructing how to cross over to the United States illegally and live there without being detected.[30] Written in January 2005, the article states that the Mexican government printed and distributed 1.5 million copies of the pamphlet in the previous month.³¹ At the time, the Mexican government conceded to publishing the pamphlet, but insisted it was not designed to encourage illegal entry from Mexico into the United States, but rather to save the lives of those who would attempt such a dangerous journey. The pamphlet also provided tips on how not to get caught once living in the United States illegally – for example, avoiding loud parties or discos that might be raided by police. Apparently, even the Mexican government couldn't have fathomed that a decade later, the United States would be overrun by Sanctuary Cities, in which asking about one's immigration status during an arrest is forbidden. Given that corruption in Mexico exacerbated between the time of the article and Trump's candidacy announcement, it is not an overreach to suggest that the pamphlet continues to circulate well among aspiring and accomplished PHIs.

At the very least, the Transparency International report, the *Times* article, and the NBPC's endorsement indicate that there is at least some merit worth exploring to the claim that "Mexico is sending" criminals to the United States. Most significantly, however, this chapter demonstrates that it is completely disingenuous and irresponsible to suggest that Donald Trump "called Mexicans 'rapists' and 'criminals.'"

CHAPTER 2
Trump Didn't Mock a Reporter's Physical Disability

The myth that was debunked in Chapter 1, that Donald Trump "called Mexicans 'rapists' and 'criminals,'" made a lasting impression on me: not only was that isolated incident false, but given how untrustworthy some media outlets can be – even ones that have a large following and a prestigious reputation – it is possible that many other things spoken and written about Trump are likely to be false too. Therefore, from the moment I realized that the "rapists and criminals" story was horribly misleading, I made it a point to evaluate information presented as fact with extra care, particularly when it had to do with Trump.

By January 23, 2016, I was already firmly in Trump's camp. So, when on that day at a rally in Iowa he made the statement that "I could stand in the middle of Fifth Avenue and shoot somebody, and I wouldn't lose any voters," I gave his words some careful thought.[32] Obviously, I realized what so many people don't – that as he so often does, he was speaking in hyperbole to make a point; in this case, that his supporters are so loyal to him, they would even forgive his shooting another person in the center of New York City.

Naturally, if Trump were to actually shoot someone other than for the purposes of self-defense or defense of a third person, say, in order to steal the person's wallet, or to avenge a verbal insult, I would no longer support him – and I'm sure almost all of his tens of millions of supporters wouldn't either. Given the degree to which the media distorts information, however, I would insist on an extremely thorough investigation and analysis as to the exact circumstances of the shooting, as I know that a lynch mob of millions would salivate at the opportunity to declare him guilty until proven innocent, and though many would claim to be fair-minded, they would either consciously or subconsciously ignore any evidence that contradicted their narrative that he was the most abominable monster on the face of the earth – or at least in the United States.

In any case, there were certainly a number of hypothetical scenarios that would cause me – back then and even to this day – to withdraw my support of President Trump, or anyone else for that matter. Of course, the more strongly I supported the individual in question, the more it would take for me to withdraw it. In Trump's case, because I thought for a number of reasons that his presidency was particularly important to our nation, not least of which that his very presence is a constant reminder of the blessing that it is possible to defeat the major party establishment duopoly with which our nation is generally afflicted, it would take a great deal for me to turn my back on him.

One such incident, however, almost caused me to do just that. Having learned my lesson from the "rapists and criminals" myth, though, I did my homework very carefully before passing judgment – and I'm very glad that I did.

While speaking at a rally in South Carolina on November 24, 2015, Trump in his typical dramatic, animated manner of blasting his critics, flailed his arms in a wild spastic motion to imitate *New York Times* reporter Serge Kovaleski.[33] Normally, that would have been run-of-the-mill Trump brashness and combativeness, the type that doesn't seem to bother many of his supporters, and often sails under the radar of even his most ardent critics, who dismissively label it as "typical." Except this time, there was a wrinkle in the story: Kovaleski has a physical disability, and by flailing his arms as he was describing him, the narrative claimed, Trump was mocking that disability. Some news outlets were more responsible than others in reporting this development. *NBC News*, for example, used the responsible headline "Donald Trump Criticized after He *Appears* to Mock

Reporter Serge Kovaleski [emphasis added]."[34] That is good, responsible journalism. It states a fact, that Trump was criticized, for *apparently* mocking Kovaleski. However, NBC's cable sisterstation MSNBC had a far more scathing and recklessly inaccurate spin: "Trump Appears to Mock a Person with Disabilities. Again."[35]

The implication is not only that Trump mocked a reporter's physical disability, but that it isn't the first time he has done such a thing. *CBS News* was off-the-charts irresponsible. Its headline read: "Donald Trump Mocks Reporter's Disability."[36] Though other media outlets danced around the subject, CBS faced it square on, and, as we will see later in this chapter, was dead wrong: that network straightforwardly reported that Trump had in fact mocked Kovaleski's disability: there was nothing "apparent" about it, obviously, the network deemed it an indisputable conclusion.

Here is where nuance is important: suppose that Walter has a prosthetic hand, and therefore can accurately be described as a person with a disability. Walter has a good job in a large accounting firm. Susan, who works with Walter, recently made fun of his fashion sense: "did you see that gawdy shirt and tie? That guy should be in the circus!" Regardless of Susan's general lack of class and dignity, it would be inaccurate to say that she made fun of a person's disability (it had nothing to do with his prosthetic hand), but, technically, she did "make fun of a person with a disability."

Similarly, if one were to watch that January 23, 2016 rally, as I have, it is clear that Trump is mocking Kovaleski. However, what many media outlets do not want you to realize is that just as Susan didn't mock Walter's disability, neither did Trump mock Kovaleski's.

That Trump mocked a person who happened to have a disability (he did) is very different from Trump having mocked that person's disability (he didn't). In fact, as we will see, it was the press, and not Trump who was insensitive to Kovaleski's disability.

Kovaleski has a condition known as arthrogryposis, which literally means a "curving of the joints."[37] In Kovaleski's case, his right wrist is curved downward, with the fingers of his right hand somewhat curled as if an open fist. But he does not flail his arms, nor does he have any sort of speech impediment.[38] That in itself should be enough to raise serious doubt about whether Trump mocked Kovaleski's disability, considering that Trump's jerking motions far more resemble a flustered individual – which is what Trump said he was conveying, than a person whose disability affects one arm, causes no spastic flailing, and in no way interferes with his speech.[39] Incidentally, the reason Trump criticized Kovaleski to begin with is because the *Washington Post* had disputed Trump's claim that "thousands" of people in New Jersey were celebrating the 9/11 attacks, yet Kovaleski had written an article for the *Post* describing such attacks.[40] Kovaleski's response, 14 years after the fact, seemed to contradict or at least not fully support his article, causing Trump to portray the journalist as very flustered.

Many skeptics, however – particularly those whose goal is to condemn Trump at any cost, and so they relentlessly pursue examples to fit the narrative – might counter by saying that Trump was aware of Kovaleski's disability and merely exaggerated it, by widening the scope of the condition to include spasmodic arm flailing. Trump said his gestures had nothing to do with Kovaleski's disability because Trump doesn't know what Kovaleski looks like nor that he has any disability.[41] Kovaleski, again breathing new life into the Trump-bashers' argument, said that he interacted with Trump between 1987 and 1993 while working as a reporter for the New York *Daily News*.[42] Let's examine that inconsistency further: Trump, even back then, was an internationally recognized celebrity, arguably greeted by hundreds of people on any given day. He was interviewed by countless reporters. It is entirely possible that Trump truly does not remember it. Consider my own personal experience, to illustrate: about a year and half ago from the date of this writing (it was in June, 2018), I met former President Bill Clinton, shook his hand, and spoke with him for a few minutes. As a presidential historian, it is an honor for me to meet any former president – even ones I didn't vote for. And so, I will never forget that moment. I am almost positive, though, that if asked, President Clinton would not recall meeting me. He met hundreds if not thousands of people that day, and probably tens of thousands more since then. How in the world would I expect that he would remember me?

Another reason it is logical for Trump not to remember Kovaleski is that back then, the reporter looked very different than he did in 2015. His participation on a World Affairs Council Panel in the late 1990s – far closer to the days when he says he knew Trump than to today – Kovaleski looked heavier, had a much fuller head of hair, and a beard, not to mention – understandably – a considerably younger-looking face.[43] Even so, the skeptics might still argue that because of Kovaleski's noticeable physical disability, he would stand out in Trump's mind. That is a fair point, except for one important detail: many of the news outlets that broadcast Kovaleski's remarks about his *Post* article did not show his arthrogrypotic right wrist, and so Trump would have no way of seeing it on television and recalling their having met about 20 years earlier.

Next, let's revisit Trump's explanation, that he was merely mimicking a generic flustered person, rather than a person with a physical disability. There is considerable evidence to confirm that Trump often flails his arms and stutters his speech – even sticking out his tongue – to mimic being discombobulated, and the other victims of his mockery have included various individuals without a physical disability, such as bankers, generals, political opponents, and even himself!

In fact, a couple of minutes after mimicking Kovaleski at that same rally, Trump again flailed his arms, this time clearly imitating the *Washington Post* as a whole, describing their refusal to stand by Kovaleski's 2011 article by exclaiming "what happened?"[44] That Trump used the plural "they" to indicate that "they hate me" further underscores that his flailing arms movement at that point was meant to describe an entire organization, not an individual.

Later in that same speech, he made a considerably less exaggerated gesture to describe the reporting of CNN correspondent Sara Murray, the arms didn't flail, but the wrists did, as did his head and neck, feigning failure or frustration.[45] Later yet, he also made the same gestures, this time more animated than those about Murray, to mimic an unnamed U.S. general who seemingly acknowledged terrorists' toughness.[46] At a February 19, 2016 rally also in South Carolina, Trump again used the same animated arm-flailing gestures to convey that one of his Republican presidential primary opponents, U.S. Senator Ted Cruz (TX), was uncomfortable about answering how he felt about waterboarding.[47]

Those refusing to let go of the theory that Trump had indeed intentionally mocked Kovaleski's disability might still be tempted to cling to a flimsy defense: that the other examples about Trump's arm-flailing all happened *after* he had made the gesture about Kovaleski. If the case of Cruz was the only other instance, then that would be a stronger argument: namely, that in the aftermath of the criticism since November, 2015 about whether Trump intended to mock a person's physical disability, Trump consciously sought cover three months later by using the same tactic against Cruz, who has no physical disability. As for Trump making that same gesture about the *Washington Post*, Sara Murray, and the general, it is theoretically possible – even if hardly plausible – that Trump intended to make fun of Kovaleski's disability, and while speaking live, instantly realized that he had made a mistake, and sought to correct it by mocking other people – ones without disabilities – in that same speech. That would require tremendous sensitivity and brain power on Trump's part, qualities that those same bashers constantly remind us that he sorely lacks.

Saving the best for last, here are three examples of Trump's arm-flailing that all happened *before* the incident about Kovaleski. The first was at that same November 24, 2015 rally (Trump apparently went on an arm-flailing stampede that day), prior to even mentioning Kovaleski, about a stumbling Marco Rubio (the U.S. Senator from Florida, who was also a 2016 Republican presidential contender) reacting to low poll numbers about his stance on immigration.[48] Next, there is the October 31, 2015 rally in Virginia, a full 24 days *before* the Kovaleski matter, during which Trump flailed his arms with limp wrists and dumbfounded speech to imitate a flustered bank president.[49]With Kovaleski not even on Trump's radar at the time, Trump made that same type of gesture about someone else.

Finally, in demonstrating that there are no limits to the objects of Trump's critiques, he even poked fun at himself in a 2005 interview with Larry

King.⁵⁰ Appearing with his then-new bride, Melania, Trump described how frustrated he would be if he was on a two-week safari vacation with no telephones; he limped his wrists and stuck out his tongue to describe a flustered version of himself.⁵¹That was a full 10 years before the Kovaleski allegation.

Before we leave this chapter, it is useful to point out again the media's sleight-of-hand. Suppose that Hal and Tom are good friends, coworkers, and avid football fans. Hal, who is confined to a wheelchair, despises the New England Patriots, whereas Tom is a diehard Patriots fan. Prior to the Super Bowl on February 3, 2019, Hal taunted Tom that Tom's beloved Patriots would be slaughtered by the Los Angeles Rams. Tom laughed and said, "we'll see." Tom was right' the Patriots won. The day after the game, Monday, Feb. 4, both men returned to work.

Typical of their mutual good-natured ribbing, Tom playfully gave Hal a hard time. "Oh, here's Hal, the Super Bowl guru! Hey, Hal, tell us again how the Rams were going to beat the Patriots. Hey, Hal, why don't we all go to the race track and you can pick the winners for us, since you're so good at it." Hal, fully expecting the daylong teasing, took the abuse like a good sport. A journalist writing: "Man Relentlessly Teases Coworker with

Disability," that would be technically correct, but extremely misleading, because it would falsely give the impression that Tom teased Hal *about* his disability, when the fact that Hal is in a wheelchair had absolutely nothing to do with it. Similarly, while Trump most definitely "made fun of a reporter with a disability," Kovaleski's arthrogryposis was completely irrelevant to the situation.

Even with all of this evidence, some may shrug their shoulders and say "big deal." Well, it is a big deal, particularly to those of us who agree with so many of Trump's policies, yet would condemn anyone who makes fun of another person's disability. Thankfully, as this chapter proves, that accusation, like so many others against Trump, is false.

CHAPTER 3
Trump Didn't Call Carly Fiorina Ugly

In Chapters 1 and 2, we debunked myths that, had they been true, would have made Donald Trump seem to be an awful human being. The saying "sticks and stones will break my bones, but names will never hurt me" aside, words can still be harmful, especially when used to insult an entire nation or to mock a person with a disability. Still inappropriate but arguably less so would be to make fun of a person's looks. This chapter is focused on debunking the myth that Trump implied that another of his 2016 Republican presidential primary challengers, Carly Fiorina, is ugly. Again, suggesting that someone is not attractive enough is certainly not good behavior, but most people would probably agree that degrading a whole nationality of people, or making fun of a person's disability, is worse. Why, then, focus on this comparatively less outrageous myth, that Trump criticized a particular woman's looks? Because of all of the misinformation in the world – on the Internet, through social media, and even (at times, especially) by prestigious media outlets – there is no particular order in which people receive it. For instance, although the Fiorina incident happened before the one about Kovaleski, which we covered in Chapter 2, someone who already believed that Trump mocked a reporter's disability would have no trouble believing he also mocked a woman's attractiveness or lack thereof. After all, the goal of many is to depict Trump as a truly despicable monster, almost always doing something horrible, vile, and offensive, and almost never being capable of doing anything noble, kind, or worthwhile. Trump is portrayed as the ideal villain in an absolute good vs. evil storyline.

The myth in question here is a sentence plucked from an almost 7000-word interview of Trump published in *Rolling Stone* on September 9, 2015, later featured in the magazine's September 24 print edition.[52] The reporter interviews Trump as he watches the news on television; when the camera pans in on Fiorina, Trump says: "look at that face. Would anyone vote for that? Can you imagine that, the face of our next president?"[53]

Surely, Trump's comment sounded negative, and there is little doubt that's exactly how he meant it. Yet there is nothing to indicate exactly what he meant by *why* someone wouldn't vote for that face; to suggest he was disparaging her looks is pure speculation. Nonetheless, it didn't take long for so many in the press to jump to that conclusion and misrepresent his comments.

Before exposing the media's assault on Trump's remark, let's explain why Fiorina was in the news to begin with. The first Republican primary debates of the 2016 presidential race took place in Ohio on August 6, 2015.[54] To accommodate the 17 candidates, there was a main debate featuring the top 10 polling candidates during prime time, with an earlier debate featuring the remaining ones. Fiorina, a former CEO of Hewlett-Packard, was widely considered the winner of the first debate which, along with her being the only woman and non-politician of the seven, gave her increased media attention.[55] As he did throughout the campaign, which resulted in his outdueling his 16 Republican competitors – which included a field of then-current or former five senators and nine governors – Trump sought to exploit opponents' weaknesses early on, before they had a chance to gain momentum. The "look at that face remark" was certainly consistent with his approach, and undoubtedly meant to give voters a negative impression of Fiorina. None of that, though, indicates that he thought she was bad-looking.

Spinning the narrative into purporting that Trump implied that Fiorina was unpleasant to look at is only part of it; many in the media tried to cash in on a twofer, linking Trump's comment to sexism and even misogyny because, after all, Fiorina is a woman. *CBS News* described Trump's remark as "derogatory about...Carly Fiorina's looks" and quickly linked the behavior to comments Trump made about another woman, then-Fox News commentator Megyn Kelly, who was a moderator in the prime time August 6 debate, in which Trump participated.[56] *The Hill* was even more blatant, writing that "the GOP front-runner added to his ever-expanding laundry list of questionable comments aimed at women with a knock at Carly Fiorina's physical appearance, and that "Trump is no stranger to accusations of sexism," and proceeded to hurl other accusations against Trump which, though they too can be disproven, did not make the cut for this book's list of 10.[57] Years later, we can see the effects of the speculation reported as historical fact in more recent articles, such as a *Business Insider* piece that described Trump's tone as one of "disgust" regarding Fiorina's face, and concluded matter-of-factly that he makes inflammatory remarks "especially regarding women."[58] Even those among Trump's biggest critics who possess an ounce of intellectual honesty can recite from memory insults Trump makes by the dozen, and it is so easily provable that most of his targets are men (probably because he has more male political rivals than female) that there is no need to elaborate here, because most readers of this book – regardless of how they feel about Trump – are likely to agree. If we ended the discussion there, without giving further credence to the voices of skeptics, we would be doing this discussion a disservice. Therefore, it is important to point out that a counterargument to Trump being an equal opportunity insulter might be: "yes, but what is sexist about his delivery is that when it comes to disparaging looks, his targets are almost always women. That's what's sexist, that he treats women as if they have to look a certain way, but not men."

Two quick examples without veering too much off topic are comments about Rand Paul and John Bolton, each remark far more conclusive about criticizing their looks than the one about Fiorina. In the September 16, 2015 Republican primary debate, U.S. Senator (KY) Rand Paul, one of Trump's GOP challengers, portrayed Trump's insults as "sophomoric," criticizing his judging people by their appearance; Trump fired back: "I never attacked him on his look, and believe me, there's plenty of subject matter right there."[59] Also, various news outlets reported that Trump refused to select John Bolton as his national security advisor (though he ultimately did so later on, and Bolton eventually resigned) because of Bolton's mustache.[60]

There is little doubt that Trump places emphasis on image, which includes personal appearance. However, that does not mean that just because he believes someone's appearance is in appropriate for a particular purpose, he is demeaning that person's appearance overall, and it certainly doesn't isolate the criticism to one particular gender (female).A CNN news analysis points to several examples of Trump's preoccupation with appearance, among them: his reference to a U.S. general as "great-looking, central casting,"; local sheriffs as "central casting...you don't have anybody in Hollywood that looks like these guys,"; and that his former national security advisor H.R. McMaster (Bolton's predecessor) "dressed like a beer salesman."[61] As the piece's writer pointed out, those appearance comments were all about men.

No clearer is Trump's preoccupation with image (which in fairness extends beyond mere physical appearance) than his choice of vice president, Mike Pence. Among others who have said as much, Chris Christie, the former governor of New Jersey who challenged Trump for the 2016 Republican nomination and was on Trump's short list for vice president, in Christie's 2019 book *Let Me Finish*.[62] Christie wrote about the conversation between Trump and him when Trump called to reveal that he was going to choose Pence, and not Christie, to be his running mate: "'Are you disappointed?' he asked. 'Of course, I'm disappointed,' I said, 'but these are your choices, not mine.' 'You've got to understand, Chris,' he said, 'he's out of Central Casting.'"[63]

My immediate reaction to Trump's "look at that face" remark about Fiorina, particularly because it was followed by "would anyone vote for that?" and more pointedly, "can you imagine that, the face of our next president?" was that he wasn't trashing her looks, but was pointing out that her looks are not presidential. Notice, he didn't say: "why would anyone *date* that," "why would anyone *marry* that," or "could you imagine that being the face of *your wife*?" He specifically said that her face was not a presidential face. I confess, I am guilty of the same act (and as we will see in a short while, I'm not alone). In my case, it wasn't about Carly Fiorina, but it most certainly has been about various other presidential hopefuls. Part of my gut reaction to a "presidential look" is that in all my years of studying voter behavior, so much of it boils down to whom voters like to see and hear. Which candidate they want to "invite into their living rooms (on the TV set) for the next four years," as the saying goes. One example that comes to mind is former Wisconsin Governor Scott Walker, who also ran for president in 2016 but gained little traction in the Republican primary. My concern about Walker's appearance (if you're reading this, Governor Walker, I do apologize – I mean no disrespect) has nothing to do with whether his looks are "good," "bad," or "in between," but rather that, to me, didn't look "presidential." In fact, I think my first reaction was: "he looks like the amiable husband on a 1990s sitcom." There is nothing wrong with his looks, and I certainly wouldn't call him homely. On the other hand, perhaps our greatest president ever – and certainly in the top three in just about every prominent ranking – is Abraham Lincoln, was widely considered to be just that: homely. In an excellent analysis of the topic, "Lincoln the Homely," Harold Holzer wrote for *Civil War* Times that Lincoln was described during this time as: "homely," and "deeply furrowed," with a "swarthy, haggard face."[64] Other quotes Holzer relays from Lincoln's time are: "something about the man was ugly, even repellent"; "a horrid-looking wretch"; and that Lincoln, asked during the famous Lincoln-Douglas debates whether he was two-faced, joked about his own appearance by replying: "if I had another face, do you think I would wear this one?" Yet with all the criticism about Lincoln's physical unattractiveness, it wasn't about him not looking "presidential."

Harry Daugherty was a prominent political operative in Ohio in the early 20th century when he first laid eyes upon Warren Harding, and couldn't shake the fact of how much Harding "looked" like a president.[65] Daugherty became Harding's campaign manager and Harding won the 1920 presidential election in a landslide.

My own doctoral dissertation (the research and writing I did in order to earn a PhD in history) is based on the impact of debates on presidential elections. Though I have studied footage of every major party general election presidential debate ever, the one in terms of image that stands out most in my mind – and the one with which most Americans are familiar – is the very first one, in 1960, between then-incumbent Vice President Richard Nixon and U.S. Senator (MA) John F. Kennedy. There are countless sources on this topic.[66] Everything seemed to go right for Kennedy on that first debate night, September 26, 1960. Ironically, a side effect of Kennedy's Addison's disease was a darkening of his skin, particularly his face, which gave him a tan that made him appear to be supremely healthy. Also, Nixon that night suffered from a fever and chills, had not shaved properly, and looked sickly in a light suit contrasted with a dark debate stage background. Those watching the debate on television thought Kennedy won by an overwhelming margin, while those listening to it on the radio (remember, this was 1960, not everyone had a television yet), not seeing the candidates, preferred Nixon and his strong, baritone voice to Kennedy's grainier New England accent, also by a very large margin.

Another example of image – and there really are endless examples – in politics was the meeting between President Reagan and Soviet Union leader Mikhail Gorbachev in Switzerland in 1985, when Reagan, who was 20 years older than Gorbachev, and not wearing a coat, greeted the Soviet leader and rushed to grab his arm as if to help him up the stairs.[67] Trump is a student of presidential history. Maybe not in the formal, scholarly sense, but that doesn't mean he is not every bit as attentive as the historians, and even more so. He understands the importance of image in world leaders. Granted, his comments about Carly Fiorina were a convenient way to take the wind out of her sails. But the mounds of evidence of his comments about appearance certainly overpower the unfounded speculation that Trump was implying that Fiorina is ugly, and absolutely debunks any notion that his criticism toward Fiorina was because she is a woman, when in fact that is obviously nothing more than a coincidence.

None of this will discourage Trump-bashers from pointing out many other instances in which they sincerely believe that Trump has been disrespectful to women. But this chapter is not meant to absolve everything Trump ever said or did since the beginning of time. Rather, the intention is to discredit the specific myth that Trump trashed Fiorina's looks and did so because she is a woman. It is an example of the book's broader theme, that Trump is not perfect – just as no human being is perfect – but that a lot of what is said about him is not true, and by the end of this book, readers hopefully will realize that the subset of his actual imperfections is much smaller than the overall set of charges and accusations against him, so many of which are false.

CHAPTER 4
Trump Didn't Refuse to Disavow David Duke

Each of the first three chapters of this book were about myths designed to generate a different type of false and negative image of Donald Trump: that he is anti-Mexican, that he makes cruel jokes about persons with disabilities, and that he is a sexist, misogynistic, male chauvinist pig. This chapter focuses on another false charge, meant to stir trouble of a different kind: white supremacy. Specifically, that Trump "refused to disavow David Duke," an infamous former Grand Wizard of the Ku Klux Klan.

In August, 2015, very early in Trump's presidential campaign, Duke signaled a favorable view of the candidate, declaring that Trump is "the best of the lot" because of his immigration policy proposals.[68] Pay careful attention to the sleight-of-hand yet again:

1) Trump's immigration policy is obviously racist
2) Which is why David Duke supports it
3) Since Duke openly supports Trump

Unless Trump actively disavows Duke at every turn (that means more than just once), then Trump, in turn, supports Duke.

First of all, I strongly object to the first accusation, for personal reasons. I, too, absolutely support Trump's position about ending illegal entry and stay in the United States. In my 2017 book, *Stop Calling Them "Immigrants,"* I make the case about why allowing the continuing phenomenon of PHIs, open border support or indifference, and Sanctuary Cities, is a serious and multifaceted threat to our national security and well-being, and that is has absolutely nothing to do with the race or nationality of the individuals in question.[69] I explain how wanting border security is like wanting a secure lock on your front door so that no trespassers will enter your property without your knowledge and permission. If you live in a neighborhood in which many residents are a different race and nationality than you, and you have a lock on your door, does that make you a racist? Of course not, because you would have a lock on your door even if the entire neighborhood was the same race and ethnicity as you.

The second allegation, that Duke supports Trump's policy because it feeds his white supremacist agenda is not necessarily untrue, but has nothing to do with why the policy is a good one and has nothing to do with white supremacy. Two people can pursue the same goal for entirely different reasons, and the reasons can vary tremendously on the scale of decency, integrity, and morality. For example, President Obama in 2012, by executive order, established Deferred Action for Childhood Arrivals, commonly known as "DACA," as a method to defer deportation for PHIs brought into the United States before age 16 who met some other requirements, such as not having had any felony or serious misdemeanor convictions.[70] Obama explained he created DACA as a temporary measure to postpone deportation of the PHIs in question, "Dreamers," until Congress would pass a more permanent measure, the Development, Relief and Education for Alien Minors (DREAM) Act.[71] In addition to Obama's legitimate concern about not penalizing individuals for coming to the United States illegally when they were too young to have any say in the matter, and in some cases too young even to remember, one can make the argument that Obama enacted DACA for self-serving political reasons. Of course, the same argument can be made about any president or politician regarding any action he or she takes. In Obama's case, the potential political gain would be increased support by immigrant communities in the United States. Nonetheless, there are also criminal individuals and enterprises that would cheer DACA for entirely different reasons. Statistically speaking, there is little doubt that among the two million or so people eligible for DACA, surely there must be some bad apples – just as in any group of two million people (whether classified by race, nationality, religion, fans of a particular sports team, etc.) there are bound to be some lawbreakers. Let us very generously say that 99.9 percent of all DACA eligible individuals are law-abiding folks who would never even think of committing a violent crime. That leaves one tenth of 1 percent of two million, which is 2000 people. Let's say even one tenth of those, 200 people, were involved in organized multinational criminal gangs. Certainly, those gang leaders would cheer DACA for the purpose of allowing another 200 gangmembers to continue to spread their criminal activity throughout the United States. (NOTE: DACA would disqualify from eligibility anyone *convicted* of a crime; that does not include actual criminals who haven't been caught yet.) To suggest, then, that because some criminal gang leaders support DACA means that Obama's purpose for endorsing it is to achieve the same goal as those gang leaders, to perpetuate more criminal activity, is ridiculous. Just because Obama wanted to give Dreamers a break – whether or not that was wise policy – obviously doesn't mean he was doing it in order to help some of them commit more crimes.

Similarly, Duke possibly may have supported Trump's emphasis on border security and reducing the number of PHIs in the United States, and that may be based on Duke's notions of white supremacy. To Duke, perhaps it means that as long as a policy results in fewer brown people in the United States, then he's all for it. But if Trump's main purpose is to secure our borders because the very notion of trespass is a threat to our national security and orderly way of life – he has so often said "if we don't have borders, we don't have a country" – then it is equally ridiculous to suggest that just because Duke supports the same goal but for white supremacist reasons, Trump must be a white supremacist doing it for those same reasons as well.[72] Therefore, to review, it is absurd to conclude that just because a racist might support a particular policy for his/her own racist reasons, the policy itself must be racist. Next, we turn to the next preposterous notion: that if Trump doesn't go out of his way to denounce David Duke every time Duke's name is mentioned in his presence, then obviously Trump must support Duke.

Turning back to the allegations in question, here is the timeline: on Wednesday, Feb. 24, 2016, Duke, on his radio show, said that although he didn't agree with everything Trump says and does, and is not formally endorsing him, "I do support his candidacy, and I support voting for him as a strategic action."[73] Notice, Duke openly declared that he was not formally endorsing Trump, and yet as we will see, many in the media spun it as an "endorsement," again misreporting the facts to suit their own narrative.

One such sloppily written story came from the *Charlotte Observer* on March 1, 2016, which mentioned "Duke's endorsement of Trump."[74] Notice more sleight-of-hand in the headline, "NASCAR CEO Endorses Donald Trump 4 Decades after Grandfather Endorsed George Wallace," a classic example of misleading readers: essentially, it implies that because a man endorsed segregationist George Wallace for president 44 years earlier than his grandson endorsed Donald Trump, that must mean Trump is a segregationist too.[75] Another perfect example of the continued polishing of that narrative is that in the same article, the writer falsely claims that Trump "has grouped Mexican immigrants in with criminals and rapists." Of course, already having read Chapter 1, we all know what a bunch of baloney that is. Equally unprofessional was the February 29, 2016 *NBC News* headline "Who Is David Duke, the White Supremacist Who *Endorsed* Donald Trump? [emphasis added]"[76] As if that blatant bit of clickbait wasn't enough – counting on the fact that many readers skim headlines, whether in print or online – and don't bother to read the entire article, the writer, Corky Siemaszko, then opens the article with: "White supremacist David Duke balked at endorsing Donald Trump last year because he believed the Republican presidential candidate was too friendly with 'the Jews.'[77] But now that Trump is the GOP front-runner, Duke has changed his tune." The writer eventually proceeds to explain in more meaningful detail that Duke did not issue a "full endorsement," but that important nuance would only capture the attention of those who bothered to read beyond the first few lines. As we discussed in the Introduction, clickbait is an important theme in all of this media misinformation.

On Thursday, Feb. 25, 2016, the day after Duke's comments on his own radio show, Trump spoke with *NBC News* reporters and said "I disavow" David Duke.[78] The following day (Friday), Trump held a press conference at which he received the endorsement of Chris Christie, who had recently dropped his own presidential bid, and who shared the podium with Trump. When asked by a reporter how he felt about David Duke's endorsement of his candidacy, Trump replied: "I didn't even know he endorsed me. David Duke endorsed me? Ok. I disavow, ok?"[79] Trump appeared annoyed by the question, because he had disavowed Duke in front of the media the day before.

To recap those three consecutive days in 2016: on February 24, Duke announced that he supported Trump, though it was not an actual endorsement. On the 25th, Trump told the media he disavows Duke. And on the 26th, the press again asks Trump to comment on Duke's endorsement, which wasn't an actual endorsement, and again Trump repeated that he disavows Duke. Why, then, was new life breathed into this non-story?

On the fourth day, Saturday, Feb. 27, Trump participated in a long-distance interview with Jake Tapper on CNN. Tapper asked if Trump would "unequivocally condemn David Duke and say you don't want his vote or other white supremacists in this election?" Trump replied that he doesn't know "anything about David Duke" or anything Tapper was talking about regarding white supremacy, or white supremacists. He continued: "I know nothing about David Duke. I know nothing about white supremacists. And so you're asking me a question that I'm supposed to be talking about people that I know nothing about." When Tapper pressed the issue, asking if Trump would "say unequivocally that you condemn them and you don't want their support," Trump answered that he'd have to look at the group in question. "I don't know what group you're talking about. You wouldn't want me to condemn a group that I know nothing about. I would have to look. If you would send me a list of the groups, I will do research."

That's all it took for the conspiracy theories to spread like wildfire and dominate the news cycle. *Time* was one of the first to get things rolling, with the headline "Donald Trump Refuses to Condemn KKK, Disavow David Duke Endorsement."[80] A 10-word double whammy whopper of a headline it was: pointing out that Trump *refuses* to disavow the KKK and Duke's *endorsement*. The more "endorsement" is substituted for support, the greater the perception becomes that Trump is the strong preference among white supremacists. And that Trump "refused" to disavow Duke conjures an image of Trump staunchly defending Duke. There is no mention in the piece that Trump disavowed Duke on each of the two days before his interview with Tapper.

The *Huffington Post's* (now *HuffPost*) condemnation was of biblical proportions: "Donald Trump Declines Three Chances To Disavow David Duke," reads like a nod to the Gospel of John (18: 13-27), describing Peter's three denials of Jesus Christ.[81] Time after time, wrote the inquisitor, Tapper gave Trump the chance to come clean and disavow, but he refused.[82] There was no mention in this one, either, about Trump's two disavowals within the previous two days. A *Washington Post* piece took the discussion to a new level, with its severely accusatory headline: "Why No One Should be Surprised that Donald Trump Didn't Disavow the KKK."[83] Considering that Americans have been hoodwinked by mass media misinformation for so long, the surprise is how many of them realize the obvious attempts to pull the wool over their eyes.

In fairness to the pursuit of truth, Trump owed the people an explanation: why did he swiftly and decisively disavow Duke on February 25th and 26th, but not on the 27th? Well, if we hear the story told by those who think most if not all of Trump supporters are white supremacists themselves, then the answer is obvious: naturally, one of Trump's insiders must have warned him that "we're going to lose all of our support if you disavow the KKK and its leaders." It would follow, (ill) logically, that Trump would then stumble and stutter to take back his disavowal of Duke as best he could. The problem with that narrative (actually, there are many problems with it – but here's the most obvious one) is that on the 28th, the day after his interview with Tapper, he tweeted a clip from his press conference the day before, and added the caption: "As I stated at the press conference on Friday regarding David Duke- I disavow."[84] And on the following day, February 29, in an interview on NBC's *Today* show, Trump said that he was given a faulty earpiece for his interview with Tapper and couldn't clearly understand what was asked of him.[85] *Today* host Savannah Guthrie pressed Trump, pointing out that he said he didn't know who David Duke was, and Trump clarified: "No, no, well, I know who he is, but I never met David Duke, so when you talk about it, I've never met David Duke." Trump's explanation was that he said he didn't know David Duke personally, not that he had never heard of David Duke. Further elaborating, Trump said "I disavowed him a day before in a major press conference, and I'm saying to myself, how many times do I have to continue to disavow people[?]" Trump reasserted that "I'm sitting in a house in Florida with a very bad earpiece they gave me, and well, what I heard was various groups. And I don't mind disavowing anybody, and I disavowed David Duke, and I disavowed him the day before at a major news conference … now I go and I sit down again, and I have a lousy earpiece that is provided by them, and frankly, he talked about groups, and I have no problem disavowing groups, but I have to know who they are. It would be very unfair to disavow a group if the group shouldn't be disavowed. Trump concluded by reaffirming that "I disavowed David Duke ... I disavowed David Duke all weekend long, on Facebook and Twitter, and it's not enough."

On Thursday, Mar. 3, a full week after Trump's original disavowal, he disavowed yet again on NBC's *Morning Joe* show, in a manner that should have erased any lingering doubt: "David Duke is a bad person, who I disavowed on numerous occasions over the years...I disavowed him. I disavowed the KKK...Do you want me to do it again for the 12th time? I disavowed him in the past, I disavow him now."[86]

Conspiracy theorists tend to dismiss the explanation presented by the accused, because they reflexively reject it as a lie. Here are the facts, once again: on February 24, 2016, David Duke said he supported Donald Trump. On the 25th and on the 26th, Trump disavowed him. On the 27th, Trump did not disavow him, but said he really didn't know him. On the 28th, 29th, and March 3, Trump disavowed him again. He says the reason he didn't disavow him on the 27th was because he couldn't hear the questions correctly, due to a faulty earpiece. Personally, I have given interviews on national television – sometimes in person, sometimes at a satellite studio, in the latter case at times without the best technology on hand. While I never had what I'd consider a "faulty" earpiece, I've had to fiddle with the volume a few times to make sure I could hear clearly. Also, I haven't done that many – I'd imagine Trump gives more national interviews in a given week than I've given in my whole life, so he's bound to have a faulty earpiece now and then. More importantly, considering the timeline of the events from February 24 through March 3 2016, what possible explanation makes more rational sense about Trump's one aberration from his consistent response in the middle of that timeline – on the 27th – than a faulty earpiece?

Fast forward to 2019, and we can see the media's con game continue: an article in *Time* notes that Trump during his campaign for president "*initially* refused to condemn the Ku Klux Klan or disavow an endorsement from former Klansman David Duke [emphasis added]."[87] The smoke-and-mirrors routine then continues by providing a link to the February 28, 2016 *Time* article we discussed a little earlier, which had not mentioned that Trump had disavowed Duke on the two consecutive days immediately preceding the Tapper interview.[88] What is truly frightening is that it's just as possible that the writer of the second article had no idea that the first was not Trump's *initial* reaction to Duke's support of him than that the writer knew all about it. Incorrect statements are either intentionally made to deceive or innocent errors. While it would be unfortunate for anyone to engage in the former, much of today's haphazard news reporting creates a distinct possibility for the latter.

Another 2019 article, which appeared in the *Atlantic*, is technically correct about Trump and Duke, though the omission of information is every bit as disinformative: "when under questioning from Jake Tapper [Trump] declined to reject an endorsement from the former KKK leader David Duke."[89] However, as we already pointed out, Duke's support of Trump was not an actual "endorsement," but the main problem with the piece is that other than that sentence, there is nothing further about Trump and Duke.

Nothing indicates the number of times Trump disavowed Duke before and after the Tapper interview. It strongly suggests that the one and only time Trump had a chance to disavow Duke, he refused to do so. Taken in the context of the piece, which is largely about white supremacy, it becomes easy to conclude that the writer is weaving a quilt by cherry picking select threads.

A couple more points ought to be made before closing this chapter. First, in the desperate attempt to show how Trump was "lying" that he didn't know David Duke, his accusers actually help to bolster his case that he disavowed David Duke, because he has done so for decades, as many pointed out by referring to his February 19, 2000 op-ed piece in the *New York Times*, "What I Saw at the Revolution," in which he explains why he did not want to align himself with the Reform Party, because it included David Duke, who is "company I do not wish to keep."[90] What is both sad and fascinating is that anyone would actually believe that Trump was trying to hide the fact that he knew who David Duke was, not only because he has denounced him for so many years, including in the *Times*, but he disavowed him on two separate occasions on national television on two consecutive days prior to the his supposedly denying he had ever heard of him.

Finally, this chapter does not address what Donald Trump *really* thinks about David Duke, deep in his heart. The reason for that is because only Trump truly knows what is inside his heart. The rest of us merely speculate. I suppose his close friends and close family members may know a great deal about what is in his heart, but I – just like the vast majority of his supporters and of his critics, am neither, and so it is not my place to make assumptions like that. The chapter narrowly focuses on the myth that "Trump refused to disavow David Duke," which is clearly another tall tale.

CHAPTER 5
Trump Didn't Call White Supremacists "Very Fine People"

This chapter is very much a continuation of the previous one insofar as the accusation has to do with white supremacy, although the situation arose in a different time and place. Some of the sources of information – both those used in this book and others – combine the accusations as part of the aforementioned quilt woven with cherrypicked threads. If the accusers can declare that "Trump refused to disavow the KKK's David Duke" and "he called white supremacists 'very fine people,'" well, that's two quick strikes against him about the same topic. Never mind that just as the first wasn't true, neither is the second.

Specifically, the scuttlebutt is that Trump called a group of Neo-Nazis and other white supremacists carrying torches and openly shouting racist and anti-Semitic slurs "very fine people." At this point in the book, it should be clear that many of the outrageous accusations made against Trump are simply not true and, as we will discover in this chapter, this one isn't either. To unravel the context properly and thoroughly, let's take a look at the backstory.

On June 17, 2015, a lone gunman entered the Emanuel African Methodist Episcopal Church in

Charleston, SC and after sitting with through the service for about an hour, opened fire, killing nine victims, all of them African-American.[91] The then-21-year-old gunman, who is white, confessed to all of the crimes, proclaiming his white supremacy as the motive.[92] He was sentenced to death and as of this writing remains on death row.[93]

After the Charleston shooting, a nationwide movement began to remove Confederate statues – remnants of the South that seceded from the Union and fought in the American Civil War in large part to uphold slavery – emerged, resulting in over 100 such statues having been removed to date, while over a thousand still remain.[94] The debate centers on whether the statues should be removed: does retaining them imply continued acceptance and honor of white supremacy and slavery, or does it signify remembrance of those who fought and lost their lives to defend their homeland (the South) and serve as a reminder of America's flawed past?[95] To the latter point, the eminent history professor Dr. Jonathan Zimmerman wrote a piece published in the New York *Daily News* titled "The Progressive Case for Keeping Confederate Statues Standing: We Shouldn't Cart away Reminders to Our White Supremacist History."[96] Zimmerman unequivocally deems Confederate statutes to be a symbol of racism past and present – not so much, if at all, an homage to any non-racist aspect of Southern history – but still insists they remain standing, or at least on the ground at the foot of replacement statues that signify triumph over racism and white supremacy; he believes removing Confederate statutes altogether erases an unpleasant but important history lesson that might otherwise never be learned.[97] Atlanta History Center President and CEO Sheffield Hale reacted to the vandalism of a statue in Atlanta featuring a Confederate soldier and a winged goddess who says to him: "cease firing – peace is proclaimed," which was placed there in 1911 to commemorate peacekeeping trips to the North by Georgia's first militia. Sheffield said: "Why is a peace monument a problem? What's wrong with peace?"[98]

Trump himself made the case for those interested in heritage, asking rhetorically whether statues of George Washington – our first president under the Constitution and widely referred to lovingly as "the father of our country," but who was a slaveowner – would also be taken down.[99] Trump's point deserves discussion, as it could potentially involve many other American icons who might not pass the muster of today's unforgivably pure standard of political correctness. Not that owning slaves ought to be excused at any point in history, but what about the case of Dwight

Eisenhower, Supreme Allied Commander in Europe during World War II and a consistently highly ranked U.S. president, considering that Operation Wetback – which deported over a million Mexican PHIs and whose name denoted an ethnic slur – took place under his presidency? [100] Shall we tear down statues of him too? Also, consider the case of the sneaker that the athletic shoe company Nike had planned to unveil during the July 4, 2019 celebrations, depicting the original Betsy Ross flag, with the 13 stars in a circle in the upper left corner.[101] Nike pulled the sneaker from market release, reportedly because of an objection by NFL quarterback-turned social activist Colin Kaepernick, who objected to the flag emblem because it had become a symbol used by white racist groups.[102] What if, one day, that sentiment extended to the current version of the American flag as well?

Consider that example, which for some would be America's worst nightmare and for others its finest hour: the far left, with its policies of political over correctness, becomes the overwhelmingly dominant force in U.S. politics, controlling all three branches of government. Suppose that those current elected officials voted to ban the American flag as we know it today, because when it was first adopted, back in 1960, there remained rampant racism in America, including blacks having to give up their seat on a bus to whites, black and white schoolchildren drinking from separate water fountains, and voting rights for African-Americans severely compromised in the South. In its place, they created a new flag, with 50 figures of Americans of all shapes, sizes, colors, and genders, holding hands as they stood upon the fallen statues of the four presidents depicted on Mount Rushmore – Washington, Thomas Jefferson, Abraham Lincoln, and Theodore Roosevelt. Suppose further that millions of Americans – including you and I – preferred to still hang versions of the old flag on our door, particularly on the Fourth of July and other patriotic holidays, and to wear clothing depicting the Old Glory we knew and saluted since childhood. Would that make us supporters of racism and white supremacy? Would we not be eligible to be considered "very fine people"?

This brings us to the question at hand. On August 11 and 12, 2017, in response to Charlottesville, VA city leaders' decision to remove a statue of Confederate General Robert E. Lee from a public park, many individuals and groups – including representatives of various white supremacist groups – decided to hold a Unite the Right rally there in protest.[103]

The protesters were met by a sizable group of counterprotesters and on the 12th in particular, violence ensued.[104] "By 10:30AM, "the groups were restless and some physical violence – pushing and shoving – had started. Police officers were stationed along the sides of the park but did not intervene. By this time, people from both sides of the rally were entering the park through the Market Street entrance and yelling at each other as they came in." Protesters were shouting Nazi slogans, and "the violence escalated, and bottles and rocks started being thrown. At 11:22AM, the police declared the assembly unlawful."

A half hour later, Gov. Terry McAuliffe declared a state of emergency. At 1:19PM, President Trump tweeted a call for an end to the violence. The worst of the violence happened at 1:42PM, when a car driven by a protester at high speed rammed into a crowd of counterprotesters, killing one and injuring 19. At 3PM, President Trump said: "We condemn in the strongest possible terms this egregious display of hatred, bigotry, and violence on many sides, on many sides. It's been going on for a long time in our country…It has no place in America." He called for a "swift restoration of law and order and the protection of innocent lives. No citizen should ever fear for their safety and security in our society. And no child should ever be afraid to go outside and play or be with their parents and have a good time." The president emphasized that "we must love each other, respect each other and cherish our history and our future together. So important. We have to respect each other. Ideally, we have to love each other."

Three days later, on August 15, Trump spoke to reporters and further criticized the violence committed by both groups: "I think there is blame on both sides. You had a group on one side that was bad. You had a group on the other side that was also very violent. Nobody wants to say that. I'll say it right now." He emphasized that "I've condemned neo-Nazis. I've condemned many different groups. Not all of those people were neo-Nazis…not all of those people were white supremacists…Many of those people were there to protest the taking down of the statue of Robert E. Lee." He expressed concern about how far the statue-removing would go: "So this week, it is Robert E. Lee…I wonder, is it George Washington next week? And is it Thomas Jefferson the week after? You know, you really do have to ask yourself, where does it stop?" The line most often repeated by Trump's character assassins, however, was when at that same press conference, in describing how some people were there objecting to statue removal but not advocating white supremacy, as well as counter protesters objecting to the statues remaining but not advocating violence, that he said "there were very fine people on both sides."[105]

Trump further elaborated that "the driver of the car is a disgrace to himself, his family, and this country. And that is, you can call it terrorism. You can call it murder...The driver of the car is a murderer. And what he did was a horrible, horrible, inexcusable thing."[106] But to a reporter's question that the alt-right was behind the attacks, Trump replied: "what about the alt-left that came charging at the, as you say, the alt-right? Do they have any semblance of guilt?...What about the fact that they came charging with clubs in their hands, swinging clubs? Do they have any problem? I think they do. As far as I'm concerned, that was a horrible, horrible day."

A headline in the *Atlantic* read that "Trump Defends White-Nationalist Protesters: 'Some Very Fine People on Both Sides.'"[107] The implication was that *all* of the protesters were "white nationalists," which for some is a synonym code word for white racists. An *ABC News* headline stated that "Trump Lashes out at 'Alt-Left' in Charlottesville, Says 'Fine People on Both Sides,'" ignoring the lashing Trump did about the hate spread by individuals and groups among the protesters.[108] As Trump and others in his administration have consistently pointed out, he meant there were "very fine people" protesting the removal of the statue, not promoting white supremacy.[109]

Some of the criticism Trump faced as a result has merit. Those who sincerely objected to his equivalency of casting blame on "both sides" because they felt one side was to blame more than the other have a point. Many of the protesters were there to spread hate, and committed illegal violence in that pursuit. Many of the counter protesters also committed illegal violence, but it was to stop the spread of hate. An apt analogy might be that the protesters were lawless criminals and the counter protesters vigilantes who, while technically breaking the law by taking law enforcement into their own hands, serve the purpose of protecting the public, not attacking it. Nonetheless, the message – as so many other messages about Trump – became outrageously distorted over time. Consider a March 2019 article in *Vanity Fair*, whose title "Guy Who Dubbed Neo-Nazis 'Very Fine People' Suddenly Concerned about Anti-Semitism," says it all.[110] In that writer's efforts to discredit Trump's commitment to combating anti-Semitism, she labeled him a hypocrite by presenting his comments from almost four years earlier grossly out of context, potentially conveying a strong message to uninformed and impressionable readers that Trump actually stood before reporters and proclaimed something to the effect of "Neo-Nazis are very fine people."[111] Another technique by disinformationists is to begin with a falsehood and place the blame on others for disputing it. Take the *Daily Beast* article, for instance, titled "Trump Supporters Now Claim He Didn't Call Charlottesville Neo-Nazis 'Very Fine People.'"[112] Apparently, that writer must have been living in a bubble: Trump supporters are not *now* "claiming" that Trump didn't call Neo-Nazis "very fine people," they've been saying it all this entire time, along with anyone else interested in objective fact-finding. The article describes a "new push" that somehow backpedals, not realizing the absurdity of the notion that Trump is somehow a Neo-Nazi supporter and proudly and openly proclaimed it.[113]

The images of white supremacists carrying torches and shouting racist venom are horrifying indeed. Many white Americans saw them and truly had no idea such behavior still existed in 21st century America, while persons of color told their unaware white counterparts: "this is what we've been trying to tell you, racism still exists!" Of course it would be inexcusable if Trump were to call such societal disruptors "very fine people," but the simultaneous replay loop of their footage while Trump utters those words is almost as inexcusable, because Trump never said any such thing about them! Hateful racism is about as bad behavior as there can be, but almost as bad is blatant distortion of the facts to falsely label innocent targets as being racist.

For the many reasons presented in this chapter, Donald Trump most certainly did not call white supremacists in general – let alone the ones in Charlottesville in 2017 – "very fine people."

HALFTIME REMINDER

Perhaps it's time to step back from the narrative for a moment and take a look at where we are, considering the book is about halfway through. No doubt, Trump supporters are grateful for a much-needed staunch defense of the president. But it is important to address the skeptics too, who include not only Trump-bashers, but individuals who haven't made up their minds. I would like to remind them that I am not going to reflexively and categorically defend every single thing that Trump ever did or ever will do. In fact, if I were to write a book titled *Things Trump Actually Did Wrong*, I'm not saying it would be a particularly thick book, but it wouldn't be one filled with blank pages, either.

This book is about debunking 10 particular myths about Trump. It doesn't mean every accusation ever made about him is false, but if readers can be open minded about their analysis of these 10, then perhaps they will at the very least appreciate that a lot of information they receive from supposedly respectable news outlets is misleading, and maybe even they will see the real Donald Trump with a fresh pair of eyes.

CHAPTER 6
Trump Didn't Brag about Committing Sexual Assault

There is a common theme to the most outrageous accusations against Trump, other than that they are false or very misleading because they are taken so drastically out of context: they often have to do with Trump's supposed attacks on anyone who is not white, male, or Christian. The myth that is the focus of this chapter extends that streak: Trump supposedly "bragged about committing sexual assault." No, he didn't.

Here is where narratives spin out of control. First, when accusing someone of bragging about committing sexual assault (or any other crime), is it important to begin with a valid definition of the alleged act. In this case, the first appropriate question would be: "what is sexual assault?" Second, it is important to understand that laws pertaining to crimes such as sexual assault typically vary from state to state. For example, there is no "American law of sexual assault." Therefore, we ought to compare the laws of various states and see if a pattern emerges where there are more common elements than differences. Then, we can apply the allegations in question (the facts as presented) to the law.

In New York, the state where Trump was born, raised, and called home most of his life, and in whose largest city, also New York, his signature Trump Tower is a world-renowned landmark and serves as his company's headquarters, codifies its statutes on criminal sex offenses in Section 130 of the New York Penal Law.[114] For the sex offenses about which Trump is being accused of bragging, an element in each is that there was no express or implied consent.[115] Different states use different legal terminology, and in New York, the actions pertaining to Trump, if in fact he committed them and did so without express or implied consent, are deemed Forcible Touching and/or Sexual Abuse. In either case, there must be no express or implied consent.

In New Jersey, where Trump has current or previous business interests, such as a golf resort and casinos, the law is clear on what constitutes sexual assault – penetration, or sexual contact with a person under age 13 when the person is at least 17.[116] Neither of those conditions apply to Trump's supposed sexual assault bragging. New Jersey also requires either physical force or coercion for sexual assault, unless the victim lacks the capacity to consent (for example, a minor).[117] The law in Florida, where Trump spends a great deal of time and in late 2019 declared his new official home state (replacing New York), has similar requirements requiring force or coercion.[118]

Generally, laws across various states make provisions for consent because, otherwise, a husband who surprised his wife with an impromptu kiss (without asking permission first) could technically be guilty of sexual assault if, for the first time ever in their relationship, she objects and presses charges. If we can agree that there are certain instances in which consent is implied – such as one cousin reaching out to hug and kiss another cousin during a family reunion without first seeking verbal consent – then we can proceed to the accusations made against Trump.

In October, 2016, just a few weeks before Election Day, the *Washington Post* broke a story that 11 years earlier, Trump was caught on an open microphone while in a bus with then-*Access Hollywood* cohost Billy Bush, talking about his attraction to women and his attempted sexual overtures.[119] The *Post* included a link to the audio transcript, in which Trump is heard but not seen inside the bus with Bush, during which Trump describes trying to put the moves on a married woman (unidentified) but…I failed…I couldn't get there."[120]

Bush then spoke of a "hot" woman outside the bus, *Days of Our Lives* actress Arianne Zucker, who would escort Trump onto that NBC soap opera's studio set, where he would make a cameo appearance. As they were about to exit the bus, Trump said that he'd "better use some Tic Tacs just in case I start kissing her. You know, I'm automatically attracted to beautiful – I just start kissing them. It's like a magnet. Just kiss. I don't even wait. And when you're a star, they let you do it. You can do anything. Grab 'em by the pu**y (slang word for vulva). You can do anything." As they exited the bus, Bush is heard laughing as Trump continued his story. Trump and Bush greeted Zucker, who at Bush's request gave Trump and then Bush a hug, as all three entered the studio. Bush continued the flirty banter, asking Zucker which of the two men she'd prefer. She joked back that she'd have to take "the fifth" on that one, and then added she'd take "both."

There is little doubt that Trump was bragging, but he was not bragging about committing sexual assault. As we confirmed above, sexual assault requires a lack of consent. The law consistently establishes that consent may be express or implied. For Trump to have been "bragging about committing sexual assault," he would have to say something to the effect of having forced himself on women and they couldn't stop him because he physically overpowered them, because he threatened to ruin their careers if they resisted, or something similar. That would be a clear case of bragging about committing sexual assault. In Trump's own words, however, the exact opposite is true. He says on tape that when you are a star, "they *let* you do it. You can do *anything* [emphasis added]."

Here is the important nuance of which many in the media are fully aware but intentionally manipulate the words to further their agenda: the question here is not whether Trump actually committed sexual assault, whether his words are appropriate behavior, or whether deep inside himself he really believes that he did commit sexual assault. We will address those questions as well. But the main question here – the myth that needs debunking – is whether he *bragged about committing sexual assault*. Because Trump clearly said that women "let" him do anything, he is in fact confirming that his celebrity status gives him such star power that women consent to his kissing and sexually touching them. Trump's explanation on that tape is that celebrity status automatically indicates implied consent, and therefore whatever sexual contact he initiates is undoubtedly consensual. Very importantly, his account to Bush that he tried to move in on a married woman but "failed," indicates that he does in fact take "no" for an answer, and by implication, only makes sexual advances when he believes the answer is "yes." Again, none of this is to pass judgment on whether or not it is correct to make such assumptions, or whether he was correct in thinking that every woman toward which he ever made a sexual advance consented to it. We'll talk about that next. The point is that it is impossible to conclude that Trump bragged about sexual assault when sexual assault requires a lack of consent – whether express or implied – and Trump by his words clearly suggests that his fame automatically triggers implied consent. To illustrate further, consider this example: Samantha owned a rather distinctive pair of sunglasses that she forgot at the beach a few weeks earlier. Diana, whom Samantha does not know, just left her beach blanket to take a dip in the water. Samantha notices a pair of sunglasses on Diana's blanket that are identical to the ones she lost. She walks over and takes them, and then leaves the beach long before Diana is done with her swim. Samantha later meets up with some friends at a nearby restaurant and tells them: "So there I was, on the beach, and I see my sunglasses on someone else's beach blanket. No one was there. I just walked over and took them back! That's one thing about me – I have eagle eyes. I am aware of even the tiniest objects." It would be entirely incorrect to suggest that Samantha "bragged about stealing" because in her own mind, the sunglasses were hers. Nonetheless, it is entirely possible that Samantha did *actually* steal the sunglasses without even realizing it, because even though she thought they were hers, they might have been a pair that Diana purchased from a store. Granted, the sunglasses were distinctive, but they weren't necessarily the only pair of their kind in the world. One can even argue that Samantha might have asked Diana where she got the sunglasses before actually taking them. All of that is irrelevant to whether Samantha actually bragged about stealing. She didn't.

Not surprisingly (at least you shouldn't be surprised at this point, particularly after reading the first five chapters of this book), the media jumped all over Trump's remarks, concluding that they amounted to "sexual assault." An October 7, 2016 piece in *U.S. News & World Report* described Trump's comments was titled "The Very Definition of Sexual Assault."[121] With a click bait thought-conforming title like that, who even needs to read the article? The author continues portraying Trump as a male chauvinist monster, who routinely fires unattractive women and insists only pretty ones should be in his presence, notes that on the day the comments were released President

Obama had signed the Sexual Assault Survivors' Rights Act (thereby implying Trump wouldn't have), and concluding with the line: "who with even an ounce of integrity could support him now?"[122] No wonder so many Trump supporters kept their preference to themselves; articles like that one equated a Trump vote to misogyny and condoning of sex crimes.

An article in the *Huffington Post* on October 9, 2016, shortly following the second general election debate between Trump and Hillary Clinton, delivered the sleight-of-hand clickbait to perfection with the headline: "Donald Trump Brushes off Sexual Assault Brag As 'Locker Room Talk.'"[123] The headline, while describing that Trump purportedly described his conversation with Bush as "locker room talk" – which someone might then expect to learn in greater detail by reading the article – the fact that it was a "sexual assault brag" is a foregone conclusion.[124] A typical reader, seeking to learn about Trump's version of the story, then dismisses – and perhaps stores in his or her brain subconsciously – the part about Trump having "bragged about committing sexual assault." The article proceeded to report about a dialogue between Trump and debate moderator Anderson Cooper of CNN: "'You described kissing women without consent, grabbing their genitals,' moderator Anderson Cooper said. 'That is sexual assault. You bragged that you have sexually assaulted women. Do you understand that?' 'I don't think you understood what was said,' the Republican nominee replied. 'This was locker room talk," Trump said. "I am not proud of it. I apologized to my family and the American people. I am not proud of it. This is locker room talk.'" Whoever wrote or permitted the article's headline was irresponsible for presenting the "sexual assault brag" as factual conclusion, and the accompanying Editor's Note was even more irresponsible: "Donald Trump regularly incites political violence and is a serial liar, rampant xenophobe, racist, misogynist and birther who has repeatedly pledged to ban all Muslims — 1.6 billion members of an entire religion — from entering the U.S." Wow! Talk about a person who really needs to read this book – assuming he or she sincerely believed that litany of falsehoods to be true. Most irresponsible of all, though, was Cooper, who as the debate moderator either intentionally or with reckless disregard concluded that the women who were the subjects of Trump's braggadocious bus stories – who we don't even know if they exist! – had been the objects of Trump's nonconsensual kissing and touching.

As is usually the case, the longer time passes regarding a specific act, the easier it is for the media to spin an opinion into an indisputable fact. Consider, for example, the April 23, 2017 article for MSNBC titled "Trump Haunted by His Record during Sexual Assault Prevention Month."[125] Quite recklessly and unprofessionally, the author practiced that same smoke-and-mirrors routine, focusing on other issues, such as Trump's stance on vaccines, and then matter-of-factly reported that Trump bragged "about committing sexual assaults."[126]

An even more recent example of the journalistic irresponsibility that leads to unhinged lunacy is the article in *Vanity Fair* dated September 25, 2018 and titled "The Awful Link between Donald Trump's Rise and Bill Cosby's Sentence."[127] The author makes the outrageous claim that celebrity comedian Bill Cosby, who was convicted of three counts of aggravated indecent assault earlier that year "would be a free man...were it not for the election of Donald Trump."[128] Clearly struggling with reality, the author wrote that: "it was Trump's election that brought into sharp relief just how few consequences there actually are for men who serially mistreat women...this realization appalled much of the country, especially its female members...a vulgar boor of a man already on his third model wife, the kind our second-wave feminist mothers would have called a male chauvinist pig...*brag[ged] on tape* about how he *sexually assaults* women...[emphasis added]." Again, the sleight-of-hand sophistry is that, while readers are challenged to accept the bizarre conclusion that Cosby never would have been convicted if the country had not have had enough of men sexually assaulting women at will, they are spoonfed the foregone conclusion that Trump "brag[ged] on tape how he sexually assaults women." Therefore, while readers are lured to analyze whether Cosby's conviction was really a byproduct of pent up frustration of how men get away with it, that Trump bragged about sexually assaulting women is relegated to the category of undisputed maxim.

Before closing the chapter, it is helpful to address Trump's explanation – if not an actual defense – of engaging in "locker room talk" with Billy Bush. To put things in perspective, Trump said "Bill Clinton has said far worse to me on the golf course — not even close," and added that there is a "big difference between words and the actions of other people...Bill Clinton has actually abused women, and Hillary has bullied, attacked and intimidated his victims."[129]

Of course, "he does it too" is not a justification, but it does tend to show that boorish behavior by men toward women did not begin with Trump, certainly will not end with him, and there are indeed far worse examples, even of locker room talk. I will point out here that I'm not a locker room talker so as not to give the impression that I can personally relate. I can't really remember what I might have said with my buddies when I was a teenager, but teenagers often say dopey things, especially when hanging out as a group. But even as early as my twenties, perpetuating, let alone initiating locker room talk was never my thing. Nonetheless I know many, many men who do that sort of thing. I know wives who blast Trump for his comments while they are unaware that their own husbands have made far more lewd and vulgar comments in my own presence! As I am not in the habit of starting trouble between couples, I wouldn't tell them (tempted though I am). By suggesting that such talk is commonplace, that Trump's version of it is actually rather mild compared to the average, and that the men who engage in it are not monsters is not to pass judgment on it, but rather to point out that it is yet another phenomenon the bashers try to pin on Trump as if he invented it.

It is also important to point out that the question here is not whether Trump *actually* committed sexual assault, only whether he actually *said* he did. Surely, no court of law would accept "celebrity status" as an absolute defense, meaning that celebrities – whether rock stars, actors, athletes, or presidents – do not have immunity to grab women however they please because it is implied that the women will consent. But it is quite possible that Trump truly believes that every time he has done that, the women in question implicitly consented. Even if, for the sake of argument, Trump secretly realized he did in fact commit sexual assault, the way he described his exploits on that tape indicate that he believed he did not, and therefore, by definition, he could not possibly have been bragging about it.

Next, what if Trump's locker room talk – like so many conversations in locker rooms – was just a lot of bluster with no factual basis? What if he bragged about exploits that never actually happened, or didn't quite happen as easily as he suggested (what if, for instance, he had to wine and dine the women in question for hours, even repeated dates, before they allowed him to kiss them or touch them intimately)? That would be the height of irony: Trump bashers so often accuse him of lying constantly, and about almost everything, but when it comes to a boast he makes that casts him in an unfavorable light, they are quick to take his word as gospel.

Finally, consider a *Washington Post* piece published on July 18, 2019 in which the author rattles off a litany of Trump Myth Greatest Hits: "Trump assailed immigrants as criminals, to the 'Access Hollywood' recording, when he bragged about sexual assault, from his appeasement of white supremacists after Charlottesville to his call for citizens serving in Congress to 'go back' to where they came from, the president has always made his values clear.[130] In addition to the "bragged about sexual assault" lie, which has been disproved in this chapter, there is the nonsense about Mexicans and white supremacists which we debunked in earlier chapters, and a sneak preview into the "go back to where they came from" deceitful portrayal, which we will disprove later in the book. It is further evidence of how the lies and distortions about Trump are often presented one after the other, as if to build a mountain of evidence against him. We have already proven six of them to be false.

CHAPTER 7
Trump Didn't Issue a Muslim Ban

The first six chapters focused on direct or indirect allegations – demonstrated to be myths – that Trump is a white supremacist, misogynist, and is inexcusably insensitive about others' physical appearance. This chapter charters into new territory: the falsehood that "Trump issued a ban on Muslims."

First, in the interest of intellectual honesty, there is an unpleasant reality that needs to be addressed up front: on December 7, 2015, Trump held a campaign rally in South Carolina, where he announced a poll that indicated that 25 percent of American Muslims supported acts of violence against civilians, and slightly more than half favored Sharia law being the law of the United States.[131] Explaining that those high percentages were very troubling, he read aloud a written statement that "Donald J. Trump is calling for a complete shutdown of Muslims entering the United States until our country's representatives can figure out what the hell is going on."[132] The floodgates of telephone calls, emails, and text messages to me began, with friends and family members admonishing me: "and you still support this person for president?!" My response then, as it would be now, was: "I disagree with that statement, but it is not a categorical ban on Muslims," because it is temporary, until we can *"figure out what the hell is going on."* I added something along the lines of "I would have said we need to ban all Muslims, Christians, Jews, Buddhists, Confucians, Zoroastrians, atheists, agnostics, Irish, German, French, Portuguese, Angolans, Laotians, Greeks, Czechs, blue-eyed people, brown-eyed people, lefthanded people, righthanded people…in other words, I would have said we need to ban *anyone and everyone* from entering the United States until we find out what the hell is going on." Trump's mistake was singling out Muslims, when in fact his larger point was that America's borders are so porous that dangerous individuals enter even through *legal* means. Trump, unfortunately, relied on a poll that has been largely debunked.[133]*PolitiFact*, for instance, mentioned another poll that had the numbers far lower, emphasizing that Muslims only accounted for about 1 percent of the American population, and that the poll on which Trump relied was unscientific.[134] Also, other sources explain that "Sharia law" is a broad set of principles that address universal virtues, such as peace and love, and only a small minority of Muslims practice an extreme draconian version of it.[135] Arguably, then, the criticism of Trump for singling out Muslims depends on considering the following premises to be false: 1) Sharia law is synonymous with supporting terrorism and other heinous acts; 2) a majority of American Muslims wants the United States to practice Sharia law; and 3) 25 percent of American Muslims condone violence against civilians. Assuming Trump considered those premises to be true, the question would be: if those same critics considered those premises to be true, would those percentages not be alarmingly high so that they would merit stricter scrutiny for any group to which they are attributed?

Granted, valid criticism against Trump could be made that he relied too hastily on an unscientific poll; a more speculative and less provable one might be that he knew the poll wasn't reliable but used it anyway to spread demagoguery and exploit fear so as to gain votes. Here's the important part: regardless of his motives or whether any poll is correct or incorrect, Trump, in that instance, did not "issue a Muslim ban." He couldn't have, because he wasn't even president yet. He merely suggested a temporary ban on Muslims.

If that's all that the whole "Muslim ban" myth was about, we could end the discussion here. But the real controversy – and the real smoke-and-mirrors ruse – happened early in Trump's presidency, when he did in fact issue a ban, via executive order. Except it wasn't a "Muslim ban" at all.

Let's begin with the story this way, for much-needed perspective: the president of the United States signed a law that placed certain travel restrictions on those who had visited Iraq, Iran, Syria, or Sudan, and two months later, his administration added Libya, Somalia, and Yemen to the list.[136] Those seven countries were identified by name as being countries of concern for possible terrorism.[137] Clearly, this is profiling. Clearly, here is a president acknowledging that he will discriminate against those seven countries. It is a measure he thought was necessary to combat terrorism. Here's the most important part: <u>that president's name was Barack Obama!</u> The law he signed was the Visa Waiver Program Improvement and Terrorist Travel Prevention Act of 2015, on December 18, 2015. Pay attention to that date: it was 11 months before Trump got anywhere near the White House, which obviously means Trump had nothing to do with it. However, 11 months is close in proximity when singling out countries for terrorism, which was a topic of Trump's focus from the day he became president.

On January 27, 2017, just one week after he took office, President Trump signed Executive Order

13769, titled "Protecting the Nation From Foreign Terrorist Entry Into the United States."[138] The order begins by explaining that "while the visa-issuance process was reviewed and amended after the September 11 attacks to better detect would-be terrorists from receiving visas, these measures did not stop attacks by foreign nationals who were admitted to the United States," and that the United States "must be vigilant during the visa-issuance process to ensure that those approved for admission do not intend to harm Americans and that they have no ties to terrorism.[139] Trump then writes that "I hereby proclaim that the immigrant and nonimmigrant entry into the United States of aliens from [the seven aforementioned countries of concern identified by the Obama Administration] would be detrimental to the interests of the United States, and I hereby suspend entry into the United States, as immigrants and nonimmigrants, of such persons for 90 days from the date of this order [with some exceptions for diplomats and foreign government representatives]." Obama's executive department had identified those seven countries and made it more difficult for individuals to travel from there to the United States, and Trump, following that same approach, temporarily suspended travel altogether for 90 days. Whether Trump went too far, not far enough, or was precisely correct in the amount of heightened scrutiny he created with the Order is a matter of debate and not one with which we need to concern ourselves here. The point is how the information was distorted to make it seem as if Trump had actually imposed a ban on Muslims.

The rampage began immediately, with the bashers rushing to declare it a "Muslim ban." A January 28 editorial in the *New York Times* was titled "Donald Trump's *Muslim Ban* is Cowardly and Dangerous [emphasis added].[140] The hocus-pocus started early too, as apparent from the headline "Trump's *Muslim Ban* Causes Turmoil within the Administration" [emphasis added] of a piece for MSNBC's "The Maddow Blog."[141] The trick, of course, is to stir the reader's curiosity about what "turmoil" might be unfolding and to subliminally and reflexively accept that Trump's Executive Order was in fact a "Muslim ban." A New York *Daily News* piece used the same gimmick: "President Trump's *Muslim Ban* Excludes Countries Linked to His Sprawling Business Empire [emphasis added]."[142] Again, a headline such as that one steers the reader to delve into how the Order affects Trump's business and that the Order was a "Muslim ban" is presented as an obvious fact.

Various legal challenges to the structure of the Order led to a revision, and then a second revision, though both were also challenged. On March 6, 2017, less than six weeks after signing the first Executive Order, Trump signed a new one into law, 13780, which removed Iraq from the list of nations of concern because the president stated that country made "firm commitments" to cooperate more substantively with the United States.[143] A little over six months later, on September 24, Trump issued Presidential Proclamation 7645, which removed Sudan from the list but added Chad, North Korea, and Venezuela.[144] The U.S. Supreme Court upheld 9645 in the case *Trump v. Hawaii* in June, 2016, putting an end to that round of litigation, though the maligning in the media continued.[145] Several articles in 2019 remained focused on describing Trump's "Muslim ban," many inserting that phrase into their click bait headlines, therefore manipulating reader opinion from the onset.[146]

Now that we've covered the particulars, let's examine more closely why this was never a *ban* in the first place, because it was a temporary delay. Next, even if it was a ban, it was not *Muslim* in nature. The "Muslim" countries that were part of Trump's original Order, as we already proved, were identified by the Obama Administration. In the defense of both Administrations, then, those countries, while containing a majority of Muslim inhabitants, are mostly not among the nations with the highest Muslim population in the world by total or by percentage. None of the top six countries (as of 2015) in terms of total Muslims – Indonesia, India, Pakistan, Bangladesh, Nigeria, and Egypt – appeared on any of Trump's travel bans.[147] Seven through 10 are Iran, Turkey, Algeria, and Iraq; though Iran is on all three bans, Iraq was only on the first, and Turkey and Algeria were on none.[148] Next, it is important to note the incredibly high *percentage* of Muslims in so many of the countries that were on none of the lists: for instance, 98 percent of Turkey is Muslim, as are 97.1 percent of Algeria, 96.4 percent of Pakistan, 95.1 percent of Egypt, 90 percent of Bangladesh, and 87.1 percent of Indonesia.

To get a good idea of approximately how many Muslims are allowed into the United States every year – because Trump's travel bans affected none of them – consider Indonesia to illustrate the example of this formula: in 2018, 77,373 visas (the primary method by which non-U.S. citizens are legally admitted into the United States) were issued for citizens of Indonesia.[149] As we already discussed, 87.1 percent of Indonesians are Muslims. Therefore, assuming a perfect correlation between immigrants and total population, the number of Muslims legally admitted into the United States from Indonesia in 2018 were 67,391. If we apply the same formula to some of the other countries we discussed, here are those totals: Turkey (84,250), Algeria (16,206), Pakistan (66,255), Egypt (63,910), and Bangladesh (34,376).[150] Adding those numbers together, approximately 332,388 Muslims were lawfully admitted into the United States just in 2018, with no attempt whatsoever by Trump to interfere. Of course, the formula is not exact: one can argue that there is no direct evidence that Muslim percentage of total population exactly correlates to Muslim percentage of those who entered the United States with visas, but there is no reason to think the percentages aren't similar. That's over 300,000 Muslims in 2018 alone, just from six countries. So many Muslims enter the United States from countries typically not thought of as "Muslim" nations: for instance, 1,494,170 visas were issued in 2018 from individuals coming from China.[151] Barely 2 percent of China's citizens are Muslim, but that still amounts to 29,883 Chinese Muslims who entered the United States legally in 2018, using the same formula. Taking all of that into consideration, if Trump's goal really was to issue a Muslim ban, he sure did a horrible job trying to accomplish that! Not to mention that

Trump actually *removed* some of the Muslim-majority countries identified by the Obama Administration and replaced them with North Korea and Venezuela, whose Muslim population is less than one person in a thousand.

The sleight-of-hand trickery by which none of us should be duped is that just because most of the countries affected by travel ban Orders have Muslim majorities does not mean the majority of Muslims all over the world are banned from the legal process of applying for admission to the United States – in fact, it's not even close. To further demonstrate the absurdity of the notion, consider that a 2001 article in *Scientific American* reported that approximately 70 to 95 percent of all human beings are righthanded.[152] Though the percentages might have changed slightly since that time, and just as the previous formula may not directly apply to prospective immigrants to the United States, few, if any, would argue against the notion that the overwhelming majority of people are righthanded. Accepting that as fact, then, it is also nearly certain that most of the citizens of the countries affected by the travel ban are righthanded. Would it be accurate, then, to suggest that Trump's Order was a "Righthanded Ban"? Of course not!

Granted, it is easy to make the counterargument that "Trump did not ever propose a temporary ban on righthanded people, but he did propose one about Muslims." And while there is merit to that argument, it is also inaccurate and irresponsible to suggest that just because Trump made a proposal at some point while campaigning for president, a policy that he officially implemented as president over a year later amounted to the same thing.

In the simplest of terms, to accuse President Trump of imposing a "Muslim ban," as so many of his bashers have done and continue to do, including media outlets that purport to provide responsible reporting, would only be true if Trump actually banned people from entering the United States *on the basis of* their Islamic faith. Trump never did that, and therefore that accusation is yet another anti-Trump myth proven to be false.

CHAPTER 8
Trump Didn't Make up Hurricane Dorian's Risk of Striking Alabama

Readers may wonder why I would choose to disprove this particular myth about Trump: that he did not fabricate a theory that Hurricane Dorian, widely considered the most ferocious storm of 2019 threatening to strike the United States, was at one point a risk for striking the state of Alabama. "So what?" the cynics might say, assuming that I ran out of accusations about Trump to disprove and had to reach for something like this. Near the end of the book, we will confirm that is not the case, because we'll mention other topics that easily could have fit in the book, but for the sake of keeping it to a short, readable size, they didn't make the list. If anything, it was far less about struggling to find 10 examples to prove false than it was to decide which 10 to select among the many. The skeptics may wonder, nonetheless, of all the things Trump has been accused of, misunderstanding a hurricane's path would certainly be among the milder ones – so why even bring it up? While that may be true, the Dorian myth is a symptom of a larger phenomenon: that Trump is stupid, unhinged, delusional, grossly misinformed, intentionally lies or has a reckless disregard for the truth, refuses to admit a mistake, or all of the above. For those reasons, and while disproving this myth does not necessarily absolve him of such criticism for everything he ever said or did or may say or do, it is yet another example of why so many Americans – and people throughout the rest of the world – are too quick to believe the worst about Trump without examining the evidence more carefully.

On September 1, 2019, a Category 5 storm named Hurricane Dorian pummeled the Bahamas and caused great concern about subsequent landfall in the Southeastern United States.[153] Dorian then weakened in its force by the time it grazed Florida and Georgia a few days later, though it did make more of an impact in the Carolinas before heading northward to Canada.[154] Rather than focus on the storm and its impact, some of those fixated on undermining Trump at any turn focused on his tweet to the nation on September 1: "In addition to Florida - South Carolina, North Carolina, Georgia, and Alabama, will most likely be hit (much) harder than anticipated. Looking like one of the largest hurricanes ever. Already category 5. BE CAREFUL! GOD BLESS EVERYONE!"[155] Like the overwhelming majority of Trump's tweets, the message was benign. Keep in mind, there are forces that spend virtually all day every day combing through everything the president says and does to find that tiny iota of controversy and exploit it to no end. And in many cases, when there is no actual controversy, they create one out of thin air – such as with his tweet about Dorian. The vicious mockery they unleashed on the president was that Alabama was never in Dorian's path at all, a conclusion that upon further investigation turned out to be false, but which they conveyed with the same arrogant certainty they do in most of their Trump-bashing.

Before we disprove this, the eighth falsehood debunked in this book, let's consider the significance of Trump's tweet and why he should have been commended for tweeting it, rather than laughed at. Fourteen years earlier, another Hurricane, Katrina, struck the Gulf Coast of the United States, ravaging a multitude of homes in its path across Louisiana, Mississippi, and Alabama, displacing hundreds of thousands of people from their homes, at an estimated damage of over $100 billion and causing over a thousand deaths.[156] Because the younger President Bush was on vacation at his ranch in Texas at the time and didn't fly back to Washington, DC until two days after the storm hit, he was perceived as detached and uncaring.[157] That many of those who lost their homes were lower-income persons of color further worsened the negative publicity, implying – very irresponsibly and incorrectly – that Bush would have been more sympathetic to their plight had they been rich and white (they downplayed that among those who lost his home was U.S. Senator [MI] and former Majority Leader Trent Lott).[158] As a result of Bush's perceived aloofness regarding Katrina, his popularity plummeted; only 47 percent believed he could be trusted in a crisis, down from 60 percent the previous year, and his overall approval rating continued to sink.[159] Quite bluntly, historian Douglas Brinkley wrote that Bush "deserved an F in crisis management."[160] That Trump would warn the residents of any states even remotely likely to have been affected by a hurricane should have been welcomed as an alert commander-in-chief firmly at the wheel of the ship. But when Trump-bashing is not only the means but the end goal, you're damned if you do and damned if you don't.

An article for CNN opened by declaring Trump as "spreading false information during an emergency situation. Not once or twice – three times."[161] Trump was "wrong" to include Alabama as part of his warning, the article continues, as that state was "never" part of the Dorian forecast, and obnoxiously concludes that Trump showed "a fundamental misunderstanding of geography."[162] At least that article didn't even bother being subtle in its deception; it spewed its venomous message openly – that Trump obviously doesn't even know where Alabama is. A piece in *Forbes* also declared Trump's forecast to be a "big mistake," and praised Alabama's National Weather Service (NWS) for issuing a subsequent tweet to calm Alabamans, letting them know that their state was not in Dorian's path after all."[163] The article lamented that probably far more people viewed Trump's original tweet than the one from NWS, implying that the president caused Alabamans needless distress by forcing them to worry about, and prepare for, a danger that never arrived. Apparently, when the goal is to discredit Trump, being overprepared is a sin.

The ridicule intensified after Trump revealed a map on September 4, showing Dorian's path, that looked to be one produced by the National Oceanic and Atmospheric Administration (NOAA) a few days earlier, except that it had a separate circle drawn to extend Dorian's path to the Florida Panhandle, Southwestern Georgia, and Southeastern Alabama.[164] Speculation spread like wildfire that Trump "doctored" the map using a Sharpie, which then inspired countless parodies about what else Trump might draw, including his likeness on Mount Rushmore.[165] As if they were Bob Woodward and Carl Bernstein blowing the lid off of the Watergate scandal, two reporters writing for the *Washington Post* (surprise, surprise) "revealed" that it was Trump himself who "forged" that weather map with a Sharpie.[166] Apparently, that's what an unnamed "Trump official" told the investigative duo 'on the condition of anonymity," as if the source was Deep Throat implicating Nixon in a coverup.[167] That *Post* article disclosed something much more important: the media's attempt to lump "Sharpiegate" with an overall pattern of Trump "lies" or exaggerations, and to psychoanalyze the president insofar as his "weakness" in not being able to admit he was wrong. The writers further cheapened their own journalistic credibility and that of the newspaper that published them by tauntingly referring to "sunny Alabama." Even when the article mentions that Trump canceled a trip to Poland to monitor the storm, it was twisted to imply that he did so not out of concern for Dorian's impact, but to vindicate his Alabama theory. Damned if you do, damned if you don't, indeed.

Before even turning to why Trump did not fabricate Alabama as potentially being in Dorian's path out of thin air, the more logical question is: why would Trump possibly even want to make it up? When Trump is scorched for overinflating the numbers when it comes to the size of his crowds or the extent of his wealth, at least there might be something to be gained. By communicating that his rallies draw large numbers of people, Trump might subconsciously plant the seed in people's minds that his ideas are worthwhile, which is why he has such a big following. If people believe he is very rich, perhaps they might have more respect for his overall ability to lead and to accomplish. In stark contrast, there is absolutely nothing Trump could have gained personally by leading anyone to believe that Alabama was in Dorian's path. Was he trying to make Dorian seem even more deadly than it was, thereby drawing attention to it and to his command over the situation? Hardly. Dorian was already incredibly dangerous, with or without Alabama, and everyone knew it. Was he trying to garner sympathy and support from Alabamans? He already has it: Alabamans voted solidly Republican in 16 of the past 17 presidential elections dating back to 1972, including supporting Trump by a whopping 62.1 percent of the vote in 2016.[168] It's not as if Alabama was a blue state, or even a swing state, and Trump thought that by showing concern for its people he could flip them over to his side; they were, and are, solidly in his camp.

Evidently, the obsession with discrediting Trump is so rampant that it has blinded those infected with it from using common sense: besides the value of taking one at his or her word as the starting point and then, if applicable, attempting to verify the truth by seeking confirmation, rather than beginning with the premise that the person must be wrong, there is also the pesky question: why would someone even bother to lie if there was absolutely nothing to be gained by it?

Finally, let's turn to why, yet again, Trump was correct. On September 6, the NOAA directly contradicted Alabama's National Weather Service (NSW), and supported Trump's claim that Alabama indeed had been forecasted to be in Dorian's path.[169] NOAA described NSW's response tweet to Trump, that Alabama was in no danger from Dorian, as "absolute terms that were inconsistent with probabilities from the best forecast products available at the time."[170] What is utterly amazing is that NSW's director then further justified his agency's counter tweet, purporting that it was necessary in order to "stop public panic."[171] If nothing else, the United States is so often overprepared for potential crises. Millions of travelers remove their shoes at airport security checkpoints because one guy way back attempted to detonate a shoe bomb on a plane. Millions more hunker down amid blizzard warnings, flocking to the supermarkets to stock up on food, buying battery-operated flashlights and radios, and spending thousands of dollars on high-end power generators, all to experience an end result of an inch or two of snowfall, merely flurries, or sometimes not even a single flake. It is ingrained in our minds to overprepare. But when Trump is the overpreparer in question, his warnings amount to "public panic," and suddenly the better message is to nonchalantly take the alerts with a grain of salt.

There is no doubt that Trump doubled down about his Dorian forecast throughout the criticism, ferociously counterpunching as he so often does. Rather than deride him for his defensiveness, one might consider an alternate perspective: perhaps if Trump had been given the benefit of the doubt to begin with, he would have had no need to be defensive in the first place. At worst, Trump had relayed a Dorian forecast that was not the most recent. If the haters and their media lackeys simply treated his message as information, maybe he would have emerged with an updated forecast that did not include Alabama. Trump's most intense opponents know that he can't stand criticism, especially when it's false. Yet they cannot resist badgering him with myths that are so easily disproven, as we have done so with eight in this book thus far. Onto the next one.

CHAPTER 9
Trump Does Not Encourage Violence at His Rallies or Elsewhere

One of the schemes by which to discredit President Trump is to perpetuate the myth that he loves fascist dictators and tries to emulate them. While I do not believe that to be the case for numerous reasons, it is not part of what this book is about, because the only way to know the answer to that question with certainty is to be absolutely sure of what is in the president's mind and heart. As I do not even know him personally at all, let alone know him well, I would not place myself in the company of so many who recklessly and irresponsibly profess to know what he's all about. This book focuses on what Trump actually said and did as opposed to what he is falsely accused of saying and doing.

Part of the storyline to advance the theory that Trump loves some of history's most evil tyrants and tries to be like them is the idea that he encourages violence, particularly at his political rallies. There is little doubt that well over 99 percent of those who voted in the 2016 presidential election never attended any of Trump's live political rallies, and certainly that number becomes even tinier when counting those who voted against him. Almost all American voters, then – as well as nonvoters both in the United States and throughout the world – are left to conclude that Trump rallies surely must be dangerous gatherings where bullying white racists intimidate – verbally and physically – anyone who dares to utter an opposing point of view. Before presenting evidence of how many in the media falsely perpetuate that perception, consider that when it comes to Trump rallies, I am among that rare 1 percent who attended several of them. Granted, most were in Pennsylvania, and so I will not pretend that I covered the Trump campaign coast to coast. Nonetheless, the Keystone State is an apt example of Trump Country, at least as perceived by outsiders. Long referred to as "Pennsyltucky" – a deriding slur to suggest that Central Pennsylvanians, and Kentuckians, are hicks and rubes – the "T" region between Philadelphia and Pittsburgh and pushing southward into Northern Maryland repositioned into the national spotlight on April 6, 2008, when then-presidential candidate Barack Obama described small-town Pennsylvanians as angry over dwindling job opportunities "cling[ing] to their guns and religion" and having "antipathy toward people who aren't like them or anti-immigrant sentiment..."[172] In 1986, while working on the gubernatorial campaign of Pennsylvania's Robert

Casey, Sr. (father of the eponymous U.S. Senator from that state) and before emerging as a campaign strategist for Bill Clinton and later a nationally recognized political commentator, James Carville took the opportunity to describe Pennsylvania as being "Paoli (a Philadelphia suburb) and Penn Hills (a Pittsburgh suburb) with Alabama in between."[173] Carville's demeaning comment, denigrating both of those states' residents, was largely paraphrased as "Philadelphia, Pittsburgh, and Alabama in the middle," and continues to serve as an example of elitist pseudointellectualism against Central Pennsylvania and similar parts of the United States dismissed as "flyover country."[174]

On a personal note, I was born, raised, and educated in New York City, and so I believe anyone would embarrass him/herself by daring to refer to me as a hayseed. Having lived for several years in Central Pennsylvania, I never encountered more wonderful, neighborly people, and less xenophobic (my immediate family and I were the only Greek-Americans in a predominantly Germanic village). I have also never heard an unkind word spoken in my presence about persons of color, and have consistently attended countless functions where blacks and Latinos and the white majority intermingled warmly and effortlessly. That many of my Pennsylvania friends and neighbors are farmers, as opposed to my New York circle of academics, does not make the former group any less logical, analytical, witty, or intelligent than the latter. In fact, it is the urban effete snobs who make fools of themselves when they make such sweeping generalizations.

Having attended many political events in my life – featuring candidates of both major parties as well as smaller ones – I've seen some exceptions to the rule. I've been offended by the Neanderthal racist poison that spewed from the lips of some attendees – but never, not once, did I hear any of that at a Trump rally. Again, I didn't go to Trump rallies all over the country, but the ones I attended weren't in Boston, Miami, or San Francisco, they were in "Pennsyltucky." I've ridden shuttle buses with masses of Trump supporters and waited on line with them to enter arenas. I got to know a lot of them, and though I attended alone, I would have felt comfortable bringing my young children there. There was no offensive language, no boorish behavior.

One Trump rally in particular, held on April 21, 2016 in Pennsylvania's capital city, Harrisburg, during the height of the hype about how Trump condones and even encourages violence, prompted me to write the newspaper article "What a Trump

Rally is Really Like" in *The National Herald*.[175] Excerpts from that article follow:

> "The most interesting and valuable piece of information I gathered from attending a Trump rally live – because I certainly hadn't seen it reported anywhere – was the explicit instructions announced prior to Trump's appearance.
>
> First, there is a preamble about how Trump deeply cares about freedom of speech, and so he is interested in protecting the rights of those who speak against him. Accordingly, the announcer continues, there is a safe haven set up outside the event, with police protection, where the protesters can voice their views without fearing any retaliation. But some choose to enter the event and disrupt it, the announcer explains. And so, 'if there is a protester who speaks out near you, do not touch the protester. Instead, hold up your Trump rally sign and shout TRUMP, TRUMP, TRUMP! and law enforcement officers will safely escort the person out of the arena.' Reporters from some of the largest media outlets – such as CNN and the Associated Press – confirmed to me that this is the announcement that precedes all of Trump's rallies. And yet, they are portrayed

as hotbeds of violence, encouraged by Trump himself. The efficiency with which this process works is amazing, considering that Trump rally attendees are not professionals in terms of crowd control. There were four disruptions throughout Trump's one-hour speech, each lasting less than 10 seconds. At the first sign of disruption, the overwhelmingly pro-Trump crowd raised their Trump signs, shouted 'Trump, Trump, Trump,' and within seconds, the police knew where to go, and swiftly removed the disruptor, as Trump rallied the crowd by saying 'Look at the police, look at how great they are – we LOVE the police, to which the crowd responded with a rallying outcry of 'USA! USA!' over and over. In one instance, Trump even told his overzealous disruptor watchers to 'leave him alone, he has no voice, I can't even hear what he's saying,' about a disruptor who couldn't be heard above the volume of the cheering crowd."[176]

I attended numerous Trump rallies in the capacity of a "civilian" or as a member of the press, and I would be remiss not to acknowledge the polite treatment I received from my fellow journalists, even as I wore a MAGA (Make America Great Again) hat to show Trump – and his legion of supporters – that not every journalist in America hates him. As I wrote in the *Herald* article, several of them who did in fact cover Trump on a daily basis, explained that the instructions about how to deal with anti-Trump protesters, including the verbiage about promoting free speech and providing a safe haven where protesters can voice their opinions, as well as to alert security by shouting "Trump! Trump! Trump!" repeatedly to identify a protester, were standard at all Trump rallies.

How, then, did the myth about Trump encouraging violence at his rallies begin? Consider a CNN montage video narrated by Ashleigh Banfield (for whom I once had immense respect long ago, when I respected that entire network), in which she falsely implies that Trump incites his followers to commit violence toward those who "oppose" Trump, with the predictably misleading clickbait headline "Mashup of Trump Praising Violence against Protesters."[177] The video then pans to Trump at a March 11, 2016 appearance in Iowa, explaining that at one of his rallies, his own security told him that there might be people in the audience with tomatoes, about whom Trump told the Iowa group "if you see someone getting ready to throw a tomato, knock the crap out of them, would you?" and that he would pay for the legal fees.[178] Laughter from the audience indicated that they recognized Trump was speaking tongue-in-cheek, not literally issuing a directive to use physical force. Granted, it is fair and reasonable to criticize a major party presidential candidate for speaking so bluntly, considering not every listener may be sophisticated enough to distinguish a figure of speech from an explicit instruction. Nonetheless, upon further reflection, Trump's comment was arguably not necessarily out of line, and certainly was not an effort to curb free speech in some fascist-like manner.

Clearly, Trump was speaking about taking preventive measures to stop behavior that, while not deadly force in itself, might lead to potentially deadly violence. Imagine someone opening his (her, *et seq.*) jacket and grabbing an object from an inner pocket to throw at Trump. At that point, Secret Service agents have absolutely no idea that it is a tomato, and they're not about to dilly-dally in what requires split-second timing, in case the object is a hand grenade. Before the protester even lets go of the tomato, he may find himself killed by a barrage of Secret Service bullets, some of which may stray and injure or kill innocent bystanders. When it comes to Secret Service, all bets are off; this is not a local police department fearful of some politician later exploiting the cause for fame and glory by staging civilian marches against it. Given a history of presidents and presidential candidates who were killed, wounded, or against whom deadly plots were foiled, the Secret Service is not about to add any more examples to that list. Bluntly put, if a Trump follower "knocked the crap out of" a potential tomato-thrower, that very well may save that person's life!

The video, evidently one-sided, shows snippets of arguments brewing at various Trump rallies, and concludes with Trump saying how he'd *like to* punch one particularly rowdy disruptor in the face. It is vital to note here that certainly there were ways by which Trump could have expressed his disdain for these disruptions without making references to physical force, and surely not in so blunt a manner. But the point that is so often lost on those who don't listen carefully is that: *this is not to excuse his behavior – rather, it is to point out how the media distorts it and makes it far worse than it is.* It's one thing to suggest that presidents (and presidential candidates) should be more mindful of the words they choose to use because they could be misconstrued, and it's quite another to accuse them of *encouraging* violence. Someone unfamiliar with the facts might think that Trump tells his followers to *initiate* violence against anyone who disagrees with him. To put it even more simply, while it might not be a great thing to proclaim one's desire to punch a troublemaker in the face, it is far worse to punch a peaceful person who has a different point of view. And many members of the press – recklessly and in some cases intentionally – falsely associate Trump with the second message.

The *New York Times*, for example, published a video on March 14, 2016 titled "Trump's History of *Encouraging* Violence," [emphasis added], which was a montage similar to the one CNN's Banfield had narrated with much of the same footage.[179] But the purported panic didn't stop then: even in Trump's fourth year in office, so-called experts compared his rallies to those of Adolf Hitler, deemed him "a danger to the public," and recommended a violence risk assessment be conducted about the president, as it was "the most urgent issue of our time." Again, the question here is not whether "I'd like to punch the guy in the face" is the best choice of words; rather, it is whether an utterance like that amounts to a fascistic, systematic campaign of using violence as a weapon to stop free speech, and is thereby the biggest threat our nation faces. The following examples are not meant to excuse such behavior by demonstrating that other presidents did it too, but it is yet another reminder that "unpresidential" behavior was not invented by Donald Trump.

There was the time, of course, when the president made what seemed to be a direct threat of physical violence not toward a disruptor, but rather toward a *Washington Post* reporter, simply for writing something unflattering about his daughter. In a heated letter, the president wrote: "It seems to me that you are a frustrated old man who wishes he could have been successful. When you write such poppy-cock as was in the back section of the paper you work for it shows conclusively that you're off the beam...some day I hope to meet you. When that happens you'll need a new nose, a lot of beefsteak for black eyes, and perhaps a [groin] supporter below!"[180] Clearly, the president not only insulted the reporter, but threatened to beat him to a pulp! For those quick to quip "well, that's typical Trump, he's so thin-skinned, so of course if someone says anything negative about his precious Ivanka, he'll threaten violence." <u>Except the president in question wasn't Donald Trump – it was Harry Truman!</u> After *Post* reporter Paul Hume wrote an unflattering review of Truman's daughter, Margaret's singing performance, Truman fired back with the threatening letter. Truman remains one of America's most admired presidents, recently ranked sixth overall among presidential historians in a C-SPAN survey.[181] As a relevant aside, the survey results were published in a *Business Insider* article on July 4, 2019, titled "These are the top 20 US Presidents (and Why You Won't Find Trump on the List)."[182] Notice the clickbait phrase "why you won't find Trump on the list." It leads one to believe that the article will describe redeeming qualities that great presidents possess and conclude that Trump obviously does not. Yet the reason Trump is not included in the survey, as the article itself points out, is because the survey does not include a president currently in office. Nonetheless, because most readers won't read past the headline, the subliminal message is successfully delivered, further feeding people's minds with how horribly unqualified Trump is.

Spreading the misinformation that Trump *encourages* or *incites* violence further helps to shape the perception that he is a fascist. An *NBC News* piece declared that Trump "uses many fascist tactics," citing his calling the media Fake News as evidence.[183] The piece concluded with the alarming warning that fascism is a threat in America that needs to be stopped now before it is too late: "Trump and the GOP use fascist tactics, but they have not yet created a fascist government. But to preserve our democracy, we have to point out that danger of fascism now, while we still can."[184] While the piece focuses on the threat of fascism and emphasizes that Trump is not the only one, it concludes, outrageously, that Trump's fascism is so obvious that elaborating on the particulars is not even necessary. Madeleine Albright, who served as secretary of state under President Clinton, referred to Trump as "the most anti-democratic president that I have studied in American history."[185] The clickbait headline of *The Hill*'s article left out the words "that I have studied," therefore giving readers the impression that Albright called Trump "the most anti-Democratic president in American history."[186] As an aside, while it can be cumbersome to interrupt a train of thought to point out example after example of misleading clickbait, it serves to remind readers of just how deep a problem this is; how the media has been poisoned by this incessant practice. Giving Albright the benefit of the doubt, perhaps she has only studied two or three presidents, and so she compares Trump to a small handful rather than to 44 other ones. Albright's reasons are "Trump's attacks on the judicial system, the electoral process and minorities as well as his attempts to undermine the press show that his instincts aren't democratic." Exactly what she means by any of that is up for debate, as it is another case of conclusions without objective evidence to support them.

An article in *New York* was comparatively less illogical, acknowledging at least that Trump is undoubtedly not a Nazi, but falling short of making that absolute claim as to whether he is a fascist, pointing less to his actions than to his rhetoric.[187] The author points to Trump's description of the "media" as being "the enemy of the people," as the apparent smoking gun.[188] So as not to further sidetrack, let's very quickly point out that Trump called the "Fake News media" the enemy of the people, not all of the media as a whole. Nonetheless, it is a valid counterargument to suggest that it is essentially the same thing, given Trump's propensity to criticize almost anything critical written or spoken about him as "Fake News." What is truly astonishing is that criticizing the media, even in Trump's over-the-top manner, is not particular to fascist ideology in any respect. If a politician who was a democrat, a socialist, a communist, or even an anarchist strongly believed that the media grossly distorted the truth to further its own agenda, would he or she necessarily be any less likely to call them "the enemy of the people" than would a fascist? That Trump respects strong leaders and that many fascists are strong leaders does not mean Trump respects fascists and much less that he is one himself. That would be like saying a person respects intelligence, and some criminals are highly intelligent, therefore the person either respects criminals, or is personally a criminal.

The *New York* piece pointed out that Trump does not lock up his political enemies. Perhaps the author should have mentioned that the president locked up his political opponents, including journalists and editors, one of whom died in jail while awaiting trial.[189] In fact, in that same instance, the president nearly tripled the amount of time a person had to live in the United States before being eligible to become an American citizen.[190] In fact, the first lady urged her husband to enact those laws, particularly so that the media would be intimidated enough not to criticize him. <u>Was it Melania? No, Abigail. Abigail Adams – wife of Founding Father and second president under the Constitution, John Adams.</u> The laws in question were the Alien and Sedition Acts, and they were supported by Adams' party, the Federalists, including retired president George Washington. Adams continues to be respected as a Founder, and Washington might very well be the most revered American president of all; there is hardly a word about either of them having been a "fascist."

Adams was far from the only president to curtail free speech. A more recent form of the late 18th century Sedition Act was the 1918 version, signed into law by President Woodrow Wilson, which stifled the American public's ability from openly declaring their opposition to the United States' participation in World War I.[191] Apparently, Secretary Albright didn't study the presidencies of Adams and Wilson.

Remember, while this chapter is about exposing Trump "encouraging" violence as a lie, the deception is linked to the larger objective of portraying the president as a fascist. That's why the previous examples involving Adams and Wilson regarding free speech were a good reminder of behavior that indeed makes Trump seem overly mild by comparison. Another example about violence, though, is more akin to Truman's threatening the reporter who gave his daughter a bad review: President Clinton, in 1996, took exception to *New York Times* columnist William Safire's reference to Clinton's wife, Hillary, being a "congenital liar," and said the appropriate response would be to punch Safire in the nose.[192]

No discussion about physical force in the United States can be complete without discussing the most devastating instance ever committed in the nation's history, the use of atomic nuclear bombs on August 6 and August 9, 1945, on that Japanese cities of Hiroshima and Nagasaki, respectively, to force that nation to surrender, thereby effectively bringing World War II to an end.[193] Before we examine the reasons for dropping those bombs and whether or not we might think they were justified, let's consider the impact: it was the first and only time any nation used nuclear weapons in war, and the damage caused both cities to be wholly destroyed, with an estimated 200,000 people dying as a result, over half of then instantly upon bombing impact.[194] The decision was made by America's commander-in-chief, President Truman, who believed that the alternative would have been a far deadlier war involving an American invasion of Japan, resulting in the deaths of hundreds of thousands of U.S. soldiers. Truman's successor, Dwight Eisenhower, years later criticized America's decision to drop the bomb, concluding that Japan could have been persuaded to surrender regardless.

A strong objection to this point might be: "how can you compare using force against an enemy during wartime to expressing a wish to punch someone in the face?" How, indeed: the latter, which never even happened, might result in a sore jaw, and at worst, a fractured bone or two, of one individual instigator. The latter *actually* caused the deaths of 200,000 innocent civilians. Again, this is not to question President Truman's judgment, only to point out that in terms of total physical force used, one instance involved deaths numbering in the hundreds of thousands, people who had nothing to do with their country's leader's decision to attack the United States; the other was words about theoretically bruising a specific individual who did instigate disruption. By the way, Presidents Adams, Wilson, Truman, and Clinton ranked 19th, 11th, 6th, and 15th respectively – all in the top 20 – of that C-SPAN survey.[195]

This brings us to the chapter's final point, that the "protesters" to whom Trump referred were not law-abiding individuals duly exercising their First Amendment right of free speech. They were lawbreakers, disrupting a peaceful gathering inside the Trump rally arenas; there were ample locations on the grounds designated for protest, but they chose to disrupt the orderly fashion of the event nonetheless. That is a violation of various laws, not least of which House Resolution 147, which makes it a crime punishable by up to one year imprisonment for disrupting an event temporarily protected by the Secret Service (which was the case at Trump rallies).[196] Incidentally, that bill, which gave the government greater authority to criminalize disruptive political protests, was signed into law by President Obama.

The examples that show the absolute difference between Trump's rhetoric theorizing the use of force to respond to violent lawbreakers and dictators committing unprovoked violence so as to silence their detractors' words are endless. Yet this chapter at least cuts to the core of the lie, that Trump *encourages* or *incites* violence. A less informed person might think that he sends out armies of supporters wearing red MAGA hats and wielding baseball bats to "bust some heads" if anyone disagrees with them, as if it were a scene from *The Sopranos, Boardwalk Empire,* or *On the Waterfront*.[197]

With nine lies about Trump exposed for their lack of credibility, we now turn to the tenth and final one of this book.

CHAPTER 10
Trump Didn't Say Four Congresswomen Should "Go Back to Their Countries"

There are many different ways by which to spread misinformation. Some of the more amateurish ones are simply to communicate information that is easily disprovable. For instance, if I say that I attended Game 7 of the 1957 National Basketball Association (NBA) Finals and I watched the Lakers defeat the Boston Celtics, that would be a lie in more ways than one: first, the Celtics didn't lose the championship that year, they won; second, the Lakers (now of Los Angeles, then of Minneapolis) weren't even in the finals – the Celtics defeated the St. Louis Hawks; and third, I couldn't have possibly gone to that game in 1957 because I wasn't even born yet!

Most lies, however, are not that easily disprovable. They involve slick use of doubletalk, vague references and, as we have exposed many times, click bait headlines. For instance, a flimsy argument can be made to give the tiniest smidgen of credibility to the statement that Trump refers to "women" as being "fat" and "dumb" because he has said that about *specific* women, such as Rosie O'Donnell.[198] In fact, using that sort of intellectual dishonesty allows anyone to extrapolate any specific statement into a condemnation of an enormous set of people (see Chapter 1, for instance, about Trump allegedly having called "Mexicans" rapists and criminals).

This type of smoke-and-mirrors dishonesty is everpresent in the tenth and final falsehood about Trump which we cover in this book: that he told four members of Congress to "go back to their home countries." As we will reveal, this is yet another example of irresponsible, unethical, and unprofessional misinformation. On July 14, 2019, President Trump issued the following tweet:

> So interesting to see "Progressive" Democrat Congresswomen, who originally came from countries whose governments are a complete and total catastrophe, the worst, most corrupt and inept anywhere in the world (if they even have a functioning government at all), now loudly and viciously telling the people of the United States, the greatest and most powerful Nation on earth, how our government is to be run. Why don't they go back and help fix the totally broken and crime infested places from which they came. Then come back and show us how it is done. These places need your help badly, you can't leave fast enough. I'm sure that Nancy Pelosi would be very happy to quickly work out free travel arrangements![199]

NOTE: it was in three consecutive parts, so here we refer to it as a single three-part tweet, though elsewhere it is described as three "tweets" (plural). Though Trump did not mention any of the "Progressive Democrat Congresswomen" by name, it was widely speculated that he was referring to four women of color elected to Congress in 2018, all solidly leftist Democrats, commonly referred to as "the Squad": Alexandria Ocasio-Cortez (NY), Ilhan Omar (MN), Ayanna Pressley (MA), and Rashida Tlaib (MI).[200] Without even knowing the context, the tweet's exact language clearly indicates that Trump: 1) identified Congresswomen as "originally" hailing from corrupt and inept countries; 2) that they "loudly and viciously" tell the American people how their government ought to be run; therefore, instead; 3) they should go back to those countries and fix them; and 4) *come back* to the United States and "show us how it's done." Before we examine this whole matter in greater detail, let's compare what Trump actually said to the generally nativist statement "go back to where you came from and stay there," which as we will disclose is what many in the media conveyed or strongly implied he said.

The phrase "go back to where you came from" generally conjures interactions in which nativists tell foreign-born persons to return to their counties of origin.[201] Although not all statements, even when their words are identical, are made with the intent to convey the same sentiment, it is difficult to argue that "go back to where you came from," to the extent that it applies to a different country (because it can apply to a different city, or even a different neighborhood), is a blanket generalization. Whatever it is about the foreigner's presence that bothers the nativist, the latter attributes it to the foreigner's home country. Here are some examples: "Don't they take showers in your country? Go back to where you came from!...You're 20 minutes late! Here in America, we start work on time! Go back to where you came from!...What kind of weird music is that? Why don't you go back to where you came from?!"...and so on. A particular foreigner's grooming, punctuality, and taste in music certainly does not represent an entire nation of people, and so it is fair to say those statements are improper overgeneralizations. Also, they are negative stereotypes. Positive ones, such as Asians are smart, French are romantic, and Italians are great cooks, are overgeneralizations nonetheless, and they do not form the basis of sound judgment, but at least they are not intended to demean. But "go back to where you came from" clearly indicates: 1) displeasure with a particular individual; 2) attribution of the displeasure to the individual's home country; and 3) a request, or even demand, that the person return to his/her home country so as to cause the displeasure to go away.

Next, to determine if the "go back to where you came from" phrase is racist depends on one's definition of racism. I learned a long time ago not to be suckered into conversations about whether so-and-so is a racist without at least first agreeing on a definition of racism. As I see it, racism is not identical to racial stereotyping, or "racialism." For the purposes of consistency, let's consider racism to mean: 1) a hatred toward a particular race; or 2) a belief that one race is superior to another. Using that standard, to ask a Japanese colleague "what's the best sushi restaurant in the area?" assuming that as a person of Japanese heritage the colleague will be an expert on the topic is more "racialism" – or a race/ethnicity-based stereotype – not racism.

Therefore, a nativist who says to a foreigner "go back to where you came from" *could* be a racist, or not. What if the belief is not necessarily hatred, but instead a belief that different cultures simply do not mix well? Imagine two openminded couples of different races whose children start dating one another, being concerned that their children will marry – not because they find anything wrong with the other race, but because the biracial children they have might face ostracism in a less tolerant environment. It would be inaccurate to label them racists. But maybe they do have a feeling of superiority over the other group – if it is not biological, but rather cultural, then "racist" is the wrong term to use. Consider this example: suppose an American says "I'd rather see people coming to live here from Switzerland than from Angola," it is easy to make the leap that he (she, *et seq.*) is a racist, because Swiss are predominantly white and Angolans mostly black. Suppose further that an openminded individual interested in a truly intellectual pursuit of the truth didn't jump to that conclusion, but instead asked the person why he preferred visitors or immigrants from Switzerland than from Angola, and received the response: "Because in *U.S. News & World Report's* 2019 rankings of the world's top 80 countries, Switzerland is number one and Angola is 78."[202] If in fact that person based his preference on *U.S. News'* rankings, whether that was or wasn't a logical way to make his decision, it would follow logically that if the rankings were reversed – with Angola number one on the list and Switzerland near the bottom at 78 – the person would prefer Angolans over Swiss to come to the United States. Therefore, it is a perceived superiority of culture, not of race.

Turning back to Trump and the Squad, even if we didn't have the evidence of his full tweet, it would be presumptuous to suggest that his disdain for the countries – which, again, remain unnamed – are based on race rather than culture. All but one of the Squad members – Omar, who is originally from Somalia – were born in the United States.[203] Ocasio-Cortez is of Latino heritage, Pressley is African-American, and Tlaib is the child of Palestinian parents, thereby rendering all four House members women of color. Next, let's consider why Trump singled them out in his remarks.

Ocasio-Cortez is probably the last person who would want to be compared to Donald Trump, and *vice versa*, but much like him, she arrived in Washington to shake up the political establishment and doesn't seem particularly concerned about filtering her emotions. In a PBS interview aired on July 13, 2018, just a few months before being elected to Congress, she seemed to threaten the continuation of capitalism in the United States, declaring that this was not always a capitalist nation and won't be in the future.[204] She also referred to the "occupation" of Palestine by Israel.[205] Trump has also shared the words of fellow Republican Lindsey Graham (U.S. Senator, SC), who said she and the other Squad members "are a bunch of communists, they hate Israel, they hate our own country, they're calling the guards along our border, the border patrol agents, concentration camp guards."[206]

On February 10, Omar defended both Tlaib and herself for their outspoken positions about the United States' relationship with Israel, tweeting that it's "all about the Benjamins."[207]
Pressley took aim at politicians of color who didn't duplicate her ideological purity, contending that "we don't need any more brown faces that don't want to be a brown voice, we don't need any more black faces that don't want to be a black voice."[208]

On July 11, 2019, three days before Trump's tweet, an article in *NPR* described a clash between the Squad and their fellow Democrat House Speaker Nancy Pelosi (CA), with Ocasio-Cortez criticizing Pelosi for singling out the Squad because of their races.[209] All of the Squad's polarizing language virtually since taking office only months earlier, including many direct attacks on Trump, prompted him to issue that tweet on July 14. Many in the media had a field day, attacking Trump on two main fronts: that he told those four women of color to go home, and that his tweet was racist. The July 15 *NPR* headline says it all: "'Go Back Where You Came from': the Long Rhetorical Roots of Trump's *Racist* Tweets [emphasis added]."[210] The author, quite audaciously, insists that Trump *meant* to say "go back to where you came from and end it there, without providing the part about "then come back and show us how it is done."[211] A July 29 article in *Time* referred to Trump's "racist tweets" about "four female lawmakers of color."[212] That article's writers apparently weren't happy enough with saddling Trump with the "racist" label; by mentioning that the lawmakers were female, they planted the seed of sexism too – just for good measure. A *Business Insider* piece provided a timeline of Trump's "racist tweets" directed at the Squad.[213] A headline in *Politico* read: "Trump Tells Dem Congresswomen: Go Back Where You Came from," and only much later in the article provides the contextual language.[214] A CNN headline described it as "Trump Tweets *Racist* Attacks at Progressive Democratic Congresswomen" [emphasis added].[215] And these are just a few of countless other examples.

It is important to note that while Trump may have criticized all four Squad members, his "go back" remarks probably do not apply to Ocasio-Cortez, who was born in the United States and whose roots are in Puerto Rico – which is a U.S. territory and whose inhabitants born there are U.S. citizens – or to Pressley, whose roots are clearly American. He probably meant Somalia, where Omar was born, and Palestinian regions, where

Tlaib's parents were born. Of course, it is easy for some to toss in the "dog whistle" argument, that Trump meant to include Ocasio-Cortez and Pressley too, to rouse the white supremacist tendencies of some of his followers. "He really meant 'go back to Puerto Rico, and go back to Africa, because America is for whites,'" they'll argue. Again, it is pointless to debate that issue, because to prove or disprove it, one would have to be able to read Trump's mind.

Further speculation might be to suggest that Trump told the Squad members to "go back" to where they came from, but didn't say the same thing about Nancy Pelosi, who is American-born with Italian roots. "That's because Italy is a white country," the naysayers might say. While that may be true (even though "white" is an overly broad term – but that's another story), Italy is also very much considered a vacation haven for many Americans, whereas Somalia and Palestine are not. In other words, suggesting that Pelosi "go back and fix her country" of Italy wouldn't make much sense. And not that the *U.S. News* country rankings is gospel, but Italy finished number 18 overall, and Palestine and Somalia didn't even make the list. None of this is meant to disparage either Palestine or Somalia; it is stated for the purpose of providing proper context to a false narrative about the president.

But what if civil unrest and other catastrophic conditions were present in Italy as well? Would Trump have included Pelosi in the "go back" category? If not, then an argument could be made for a racist element. But that is a big if, with absolutely no credible evidence to support it – only irrational anti-Trump hysteria.

In any case, no matter what Trump really believes deep down, to suggest that he told four Congresswomen to "go back to where they came from" as in to stay there permanently because we don't want their kind here, is completely inaccurate. Ten lies or out-of-context misleading statements, 10 proven false.

CONCLUSION
What This Book Proves

From the onset of this book, I made clear that by "lies" I meant not only outright falsehoods, but also misleading out-of-context statements that tricked the American people into accepting incorrect conclusions. There were others that could have been included as well: that he started the birther conspiracy about Barack Obama (he didn't), that his MAGA hats are really made in China (they're not), that his pompadour hairstyle is really a wig (it's not), or that he stole from a children's cancer charity (of course that's a lie!). But the 10 featured in this book were chosen for a purpose, not least of which because to this day, stories appear that routinely blast the president on many of these all at once, treating them like foregone conclusions, rather than the intentionally or recklessly told distortions that they are.

This book is not going to change everyone's mind about Donald Trump. Also, being that it was written during Trump's presidency, there is still much more American and world history that Trump will impact that isn't covered here. A hundred years from now, historians may rank Trump as the best president ever, or the worst, or somewhere in the wide range in between.

If readers get their hands on this book then, in 2120, they may wonder: "why in the world did anyone ever vote *for* Donald Trump?" or "why in the world did anyone ever vote *against* him?" No matter what the answer, what this book concludes will stand the test of time.

Whatever Trump is, was, or will be, 10 things are clear:1) he did not make a general statement that Mexicans are rapists and criminals; 2) although he mocked a reporter who happens to have a physical disability, he mocked him for a reason that had nothing to do with the disability; 3) his reference to Carly Fiorina's face did not suggest that she was ugly; 4) he did not refuse to disavow David Duke – in fact, he disavowed him many times; 5) he did not refer to white supremacists as "very fine people"; 6) he did not brag about committing sexual assault; 7) he did not impose a "Muslim ban"; 8) he was not wrong about the fact that there was a reported risk about Hurricane Dorian striking Alabama; 9) he does not encourage violence; and 10) he did not suggest that four Congresswomen of color go back to their countries in terms of staying there and never coming back.

Many folks, prior to reading this book, did not know that any of these 10 accusations, let alone all of them, were false. Maybe now they'll think twice before believing what they hear or read about

Trump without investigating it further. Or, maybe they still have plenty of reasons to dislike Trump based on *true* statements about him, personally or politically. Maybe it offends them that he's been married three times; or that he has had a decades-long reputation for having an eye for the ladies. Perhaps his confrontational style bothers them, and they'd rather be polite and lose than ruthless and win. Maybe they prefer open borders, Sanctuary Cities, a Green New Deal, a single payer healthcare system, and a Supreme Court that focuses more on social justice activism than judicial restraint. Maybe they are "Never-Trumpers," who are worried about his trade policies and don't think he goes to church often enough. In that case, they will not become Trump supporters as a result of having read this book. But, hopefully, they too will be openminded and evaluate Trump on a case-by-case basis, rather than blindly following the Trump-bashers to condemn him at every turn, whether justified or not.

That is the purpose of this book: to record a slice of American presidential history as accurately as possible.

AFTERWORD
Is Trump a Racist? Speculation vs. Fact

Is Donald Trump really a racist? Does he hate blacks, foreigners, Muslims, gays? Would he rather live in a place where he sees nothing but American-born, heterosexual white Christians all around him? I tend to think not, but my guess is mere speculation, no more or less credible than the speculation by those who think yes. Although I based this book on factual conclusions rather than speculation, I'll take a moment to explain why my guess is that Trump is not a racist. It's not because I don't want him to be. I don't, but I wouldn't form my opinion on what he is based on what I *wish* he is or isn't.

For all intents and purposes, Donald Trump has all the money to live his life exactly as he wants to. If I had Trump's billions, I would avoid cold, icy, winters. Always. I would make sure to spend most of my time in some of the best warm-weather places in the world, and would only travel to cold-weather places in the summer. And I'd surround myself with people I wanted around me – I'd even buy them nice houses to entice them to move near me. That's what I could do with Trump's billions.

Therefore, if Trump really hated persons of color, or other groups, why on earth would he have spent all those years in New York City? Manhattan is loaded with persons of all shapes, sizes, colors, religions, and sexual orientations; it is the last place on earth where one who seeks the company of only American-born, heterosexual white Christians would ever choose to live. Also, even though Trump was born and raised in Queens, he spent most of his life in Manhattan. I believe Manhattan shaped him, just as it shaped me. I never saw "my own kind" in terms of racial, ethnic, or religious demographics. I think most New Yorkers don't either.

Those are the reasons that I tend to think Trump is not a racist. But because I speculate, I don't raise the accusation that Trump is a racist to the level of "lie," because I cannot effectively disprove it. As I mentioned many times throughout the book, to really know what a person is – whether racist, anti-Semitic, sexist, Islamophobic, homophobic, xenophobic, etc. – you really have to be able to read that person's mind or live in that person's heart. Considering that as of this writing, I haven't even met Donald Trump, it would be absurdly irresponsible of me to speculate about what's on his mind and in his heart – never mind that thousands upon thousands of Trump bashers who never met him either, speak about him with such authority as if they've known him all of his life.

EPILOGUE
After the Impeachment

On December 18, 2019, the Democratic-controlled U.S. House of Representatives formally impeached President Trump on two counts: abuse of power and obstruction of Congress.[216] U.S. Senator (WI) Ron Johnson eloquently asserted in his November 18, 2019 letter to Republican House Members Jim Jordan (OH) and Devin Nunes (CA), "a concerted, and possibly coordinated, effort to sabotage the Trump administration…probably began in earnest the day after the 2016 presidential election."[217] Johnson cited comments made 10 days after Trump's inauguration (January 30, 2017) by Mark Zaid, an attorney for the whistleblower whose comments ultimately ignited the impeachment, that "#coup has started. First of many steps. #rebellion. #Impeachment will follow ultimately."[218] As Senator Johnson described, there were many reasons to believe that it was the goal of many Democrats to impeach the new president virtually from the moment he took office. A two-year investigation followed into whether Trump "colluded with Russia" to influence the 2016 election, concluding with Special Counsel Robert Mueller declaring that he and his team could find no evidence connecting President Trump to any such wrongdoing. But that didn't stop those who were hell-bent on cutting Trump's presidency short.

After fighting off frenzied calls by the Squad and their supporters to impeach Trump by telling them – and her constituents – that "he's not worth it," Speaker Pelosi nonetheless succumbed to the pressure and moved forward with the two impeachment articles.[219] The charges stemmed from a phonecall Trump made to the newly elected president of Ukraine, Volodymyr Zelensky on July 25, 2019, during which Trump asked Zelensky to investigate corruption into Ukraine, and among other details mentioned a specific example involving Hunter Biden whose father, Joe, at the time he was Vice President of the United States pressured Ukraine to halt an investigation into the company for which his son worked.[220] Because Biden is one of about 25 or so candidates seeking the 2020 Democratic presidential nomination, the media immediately spun the story that Trump used his influence as president to pressure a foreign country to investigate one of Trump's political rivals, and further twisted the story to allude that Trump thereby was asking a foreign nation to interfere in the 2020 election.[221]

Johnson's letter is entirely consistent with the transcript of the Trump-Zelensky phonecall, insofar as the president demonstrates his longstanding concern that Ukraine has been corrupt and therefore there needs to be further probing into its government before Trump would release U.S. aid to that country, and that American allies, namely, European nations, haven't done enough to pay their fair share in terms of giving monetary aid to Ukraine.[222] Citing his conversation with German Chancellor Angela Merkel, Trump told Johnson, the latter wrote, that we Americans are "schmucks" because we sit by idly as U.S. allies continue to ignore funding geopolitical allies because they know the United States will fund them itself.[223]

On February 5, after a brief trial, the U.S. Senate acquitted President Trump on both counts rather easily; while a supermajority was needed to convict, the Senate did not even reach a majority, as more Senators voted to acquit than to convict.[224] As this book went to press, President Trump was riding the momentum of acquittal, heading into the final nine months before Election Day 2020.

Trump's (first) impeachment saga (I say "first" because there seems to be no end to his haters' relentlessness to unseat him) was worth including in this book for one reason: not because it requires a chapter, but because it provides yet another example of journalistic malpractice. Essentially, a majority of Senators concluded that it is perfectly proper for a sitting president to want a better understanding of the corruption level of a nation to which he would give hundreds of millions of dollars in aid, and that such investigation is not categorically invalid just because the investigation would involve an individual who happens to be his political rival. The question, then, as to why Trump wanted such an investigation (which, by the way, didn't take place, even though the aid was released to Ukraine) – for a genuine desire to investigate corruption or an opportunity to weaken a political rival's campaign – is speculative, and speculation is not what this book is about. Rather, the media's spin that Trump wanted "an investigation of a political rival," rather than an investigation *of corruption, which happened to involve a political rival*, is exactly the type of thought-control doubletalk this book focuses on identifying, debunking, and shaming.

President Trump has been called a "fascist" for referring to the American media as "the enemy of the people." Well, any American should be called unpatriotic and irresponsible who doesn't stand up and recognize that many members of today's media are enemies of truth, integrity, professionalism, and all of the other canons of good and noble journalism.

ACKNOWLEDGMENTS

Now and always, the greatest riches of life are the love and support of family and friends – my wife first and foremost.. Thank you – all of you.

Special thanks to Marjorie Henise for a good, close proofread, and last but certainly not least, to Congressman Gus Bilirakis for writing the Foreword, and for his tireless and influential role in helping to Make America Great Again.

ENDNOTES

[1] Daniel Leip's Presidential Atlas, retrieved on September 21, 2019, http://uselectionatlas.org/RESULTS/national.php?year=1984.
[2] Donald Trump, *The America We Deserve*, Los Angeles, CA: Renaissance Books, 2000.
[3] Leip, retrieved on September 21, 2019, http://uselectionatlas.org/RESULTS/index.html.
[4] Constantinos E. Scaros, *Grumpy Old Party*, revised edition, KDP: Seattle, WA, 2017.
[5] Lars Willnat and David H. Weaver, "The American Journalist in the Digital Age," Bloomington, IN: Indiana University School of Journalism, 14.
[6] Dave Levinthal and Michael Beckel, "Journalists Shower Hillary Clinton with Campaign Cash," *Center for Public Integrity*, October 17, 2016, retrieved on September 22, 2019, http://publicintegrity.org/federal-politics/journalists-shower-hillary-clinton-with-campaign-cash.
[7] Bob Kohn, *Journalistic Fraud: How the New York Times Distorts the News and Why it Can No Longer Be Trusted*, Nashville, TN: WND Books, 2003.
[8] Eric Alterman, "Bush's War on the Press," *The Nation*, April 21, 2005, retrieved on September 22, 2019, http://www.thenation.com/article/bushs-war-press.
[9] Katherine Q. Seelye, "Flash! President Bush Says He Reads Papers," *New York Times*, C6, December 25, 2006.
[10] *Ibid.*
[11] David E. Sanger, ""Panel Urges Basic Shift in U.S. Policy in Iraq," *New York Times*, December 7, 2006, A1.
[12] *Ibid.*
[13] Editorial Board, "Hillary Clinton for President." *Washington Post*, October 13, 2016, retrieved on October 19, 2019, http://www.washingtonpost.com/opinions/hillary-clinton-for-president/2016/10/12/665f9698-8caf-11e6-bf8a-3d26847eeed4_story.html.
[14] *Boston Globe*, April 10, 2016, 1.
[15] *Ibid.*
[16] Editorial Board, "Damn Right We're with Her," *New York Daily News*, November 1, 2016, retrieved on October 3, 2019, http://interactive.nydailynews.com/2016/11/daily-news-editorial-hillary-clinton-for-president.
[17] Editorial Board, "These Are Unsettling Times that Require a Steady Hand: That's Hillary Clinton," *Houston Chronicle*, November 3, 2016, retrieved on October 3, 2019,

http://www.chron.com/opinion/recommendations/article/For-Hillary-Clinton-8650345.php.

[18] Editorial Board, "Endorsement: Hillary Clinton is the Only Choice to Move America Ahead," *Arizona Republic*, September 27, 2016, retrieved on October 4, 2019, http://www.azcentral.com/story/opinion/editorial/2016/09/27/hillary-clinton-endorsement/91198668.

[19] Trump, 100.

[20] *Ibid.*

[21] "Media Use and Evaluation," *Gallup*, retrieved on October 24, 2019, http://news.gallup.com/poll/1663/media-use-evaluation.aspx.

[22] *Ibid.*

[23] *Ibid.*

[24] *Ibid.*

[25] Time Staff, "Here's Donald Trump's Presidential Announcement Speech," *Time*, June 16, 2015, retrieved on November 6, 2019, http://time.com/3923128/donald-trump-announcement-speech.

[26] See, for example, Michelle Mark, "Trump Just Referred to One of His Most Infamous Campaign Comments: Calling Mexicans 'rapists,'"*Business Insider*, April 5, 2018, retrieved on November 16, 2019, http://www.businessinsider.com/trump-mexicans-rapists-remark-reference-2018-4.

[27] Time Staff.

[28] National Border Patrol Council, "National Border Patrol Council Endorses Donald Trump for President," March 30, 2016, retrieved on November 16, 2016, http://bpunion.org/press-releases/national-border-patrol-council-endorses-donald-trump-for-president.

[29] "Corruption Perceptions Index 2015 (as amended)," Transparency International, September 13, 2017, retrieved on November 24, 2019, http://www.transparency.org/cpi2015.

[30] James C. McKinley, Jr., "A Mexican Manual for Illegal Migrants Upsets Some in U.S.," *New York Times*, January 6, 2005, retrieved on November 24, 2019, http://www.nytimes.com/2005/01/06/world/americas/a-mexican-manual-for-illegal-migrants-upsets-some-in-us.html.

[31] *Ibid, et seq.*

[32] Colin Dwyer, "Donald Trump" 'I Could…Shoot Somebody, and I Wouldn't Lose Any Voters," *NPR*, January 23, 2016, retrieved on November 25, 2016, http://www.npr.org/sections/thetwo-way/2016/01/23/464129029/donald-trump-i-could-shoot-somebody-and-i-wouldnt-lose-any-voters.

[33] Live Stream Video, "Trump Attends Rally in SC," *Washington Post*, November 24, 2015, retrieved on November 25, 2019, http://www.youtube.com/user/WashingtonPost/search?query=Trump+November+24.

[34] Daniel Arkin, "Donald Trump Criticized after He Appears to Mock Reporter Serge Kovaleski," *NBC News*, November 26, 2015, retrieved on November 25, 2019, http://www.nbcnews.com/politics/2016-election/new-york-times-slams-donald-trump-after-he-appears-mock-n470016.

[35] Tony Dokoupil and Joy Y. Wang, "Trump Appears to Mock a Person with Disabilities. Again," *MSNBC*, November 26, 2015, retrieved on November 25, 2019, http://www.msnbc.com/msnbc/trump-mocks-person-disability-again.

[36] Sopan Deb, "Donald Trump Mocks Reporter's Disability," *CBS News*, November 25, 2015, retrieved on November 25, 2019, http://www.cbsnews.com/news/donald-trump-mocks-reporters-disability.

[37] See, for example, "Washington Post Reporters Discussing Foreign Affairs," C-SPAN, May 14, 1998, retrieved on November 27, 2019, http://www.c-span.org/video/?105764-1/great-decisions-world.

[38] *Ibid.*

[39] Time Staff, "Donald Trump Says He Didn't Mock Journalist with Disability," *Time*, November 27, 2015, retrieved on November 27, 2019, http://time.com/4128128/donald-trump-kovaleski-journalist-disability.

[40] *Ibid, et seq.*

[41] Dokoupil.

[42] *Ibid.*

[43] C-SPAN.

[44] *Washington Post*, November 24, 2015.

[45] *Ibid.*

[46] *Ibid.*

[47] "Donald Trump Campaign Rally in Charleston, South Carolina," C-SPAN, February 19, 2016, retrieved on November 27, 2019, http://www.c-span.org/video/?404947-1/donald-trump-campaign-rally-charleston-south-carolina.

[48] *Washington Post*, November 24, 2015.

[49] "Even More Video Evidence Trump Did Not Mock Reporter's Disability," *Catholics4Trump*, September 8, 2016, retrieved on November 27, 2019, http://www.catholics4trump.com/even-more-video-evidence-trump-did-not-mock-reporters-disability.

[50] Larry King, "Donald and Melania as Newlyweds," *CNN*, May 17, 2005, retrieved on November 27, 2019, http://www.cnn.com/videos/entertainment/2016/05/06/donald-trump-melania-trump-2005-entire-larry-king-live-intv.cnn.

[51] *Ibid.*

[52] Paul Solotaroff, "Trump Seriously: on the Trail with the GOP's Tough Guy," *Rolling Stone*, September 9, 2015, retrieved on November 28,

2019, http://www.rollingstone.com/politics/politics-news/trump-seriously-on-the-trail-with-the-gops-tough-guy-41447.
[53] *Ibid.*
[54] Patrick O'Connor, Janet Hook, *et al.*, "GOP Candidates Hold Raucous Debate," *Wall Street Journal*, August 6, 2015, retrieved on November 28, 2019, http://www.wsj.com/articles/gop-candidates-hold-raucous-debate-1438914703.
[55] *Ibid.* Hewlett-Packard was a multinational technology company and is now known as HP, Inc.
[56] Ellen Uchimiya, "Donald Trump Insults Carly Fiorina's Appearance," *CBS News*, September 10, 2015, retrieved on November 28, 2019, https://www.cbsnews.com/news/donald-trump-insults-carly-fiorinas-appearance.
[57] Neetzan Zimmerman, "Trump Mocks Fiorina's Physical Appearance: 'Look at That Face!'" *The Hill*, September 9, 2015, retrieved on November 28, 2019, http://thehill.com/blogs/blog-briefing-room/253178-trump-insults-fiorinas-physical-appearance-look-at-that-face.
[58] Bryan Logan, "Donald Trump Mocks Rival Carly Fiorina's Face: 'look at that face, would anyone vote for that?'" *Business Insider*, September 9, 2015, retrieved on November 28, 2019, http://www.businessinsider.com/donald-trump-carly-fiorina-face-insult-2015-9.
[59] Ryan Teague Beckwith, 'Transcript: Read the Full Text of the Second Republican Debate," *Time*, September 17, 2015, retrieved on http://time.com/4037239/second-republican-debate-transcript-cnn.
[60] Brennan Weiss, "'His Mustache is a Problem': Trump Reportedly Soured on John Bolton for a Top Cabinet Position Because of His Looks," *Business Insider*, January 3, 2018, retrieved on November 28, 2019, http://www.businessinsider.com/john-bolton-mustache-cost-him-trump-cabinet-post-fire-and-fury-claims-2018-1.
[61] Daniel Dale: "'Central Casting': Trump is Talking More than Ever about Men's Looks," *CNN*, August 13, 2019, retrieved on November 28, 2019, http://www.cnn.com/2019/08/13/politics/central-casting-trump-is-talking-more-than-ever-about-mens-looks/index.html.
[62] Christopher J. Christie, *Let Me Finish*, Hachette Book Group: New York, NY, 2019, p. 288.
[63] *Ibid.*
[64] Harold Holzer, "Lincoln the Homely," *HistoryNet*, February, 2008, retrieved on November 28, 2019, http://www.historynet.com/lincoln-the-homely.htm.
[65] John Dean, *Warren Harding*, Times Books: New York, NY, 2004, p. 33.
[66] See, for example, Editors, "The Kennedy-Nixon Debates," *The History Channel*, September 21, 2010, retrieved on November 28,

2019, http://www.history.com/topics/us-presidents/kennedy-nixon-debates.
[67] Stephen F. Knott and Jeffrey L. Chidester, *At Reagan's Side*, Plymouth, UK: Rowman& Littlefield, 2009, 189.
[68] Jeremy Diamond, "David Duke on Trump: He's 'the Best of the Lot,'" *CNN*, August 25, 2015, retrieved on November 29, 2019, http://www.cnn.com/2015/08/25/politics/david-duke-donald-trump-immigration.
[69] Scaros, *Stop Calling Them "Immigrants,"* Seattle, WA: KDP, 2017.
[70] Transcript, "Remarks by the President on Immigration," White House, June 15, 2012, retrieved on November 29, 2019, http://obamawhitehouse.archives.gov/the-press-office/2012/06/15/remarks-president-immigration.
[71] *Ibid*.
[72] Trump, Twitter, November 12, 2015, retrieved on November 29, 2019, http://twitter.com/realdonaldtrump/status/664787273184108545?lang=en.
[73] Josh Hafner, "Former Ku Klux Klan Leader Declares Support for Donald Trump," *USA Today*, February 25, 2016, retrieved on http://www.usatoday.com/story/news/politics/onpolitics/2016/02/25/david-duke-trump/80953384.
[74] Jonathan Jones, "NASCAR CEO Endorses Donald Trump 4 Decades after Grandfather Endorsed George Wallace," *Charlotte Observer*, March 1, 2016, retrieved on November 29, 2016, http://www.charlotteobserver.com/sports/nascar-auto-racing/thatsracin/article63382092.html.
[75] *Ibid*.
[76] Corky Siemaszko, "Who Is David Duke, the White Supremacist Who Endorsed Donald Trump?" *NBC News*, February 29, 2016, retrieved on November 29, 2017, http://www.nbcnews.com/news/us-news/who-david-duke-white-supremacist-who-endorsed-donald-trump-n528141.
[77] *Ibid, et seq*.
[78] Jane C. Timm, "Donald Trump's History of Talking about David Duke and White Supremacists," MSNBC, February 29, 2016, retrieved on November 29, 2019, http://www.msnbc.com/msnbc/donald-trumps-history-talking-about-david-duke-and-white-supremacists
[79] *Ibid, et seq*.
[80] Melissa Chan, "Donald Trump Refuses to Condemn KKK, Disavow David Duke Endorsement," *Time*, February 28, 2016, retrieved on November 29, 2019, http://time.com/4240268/donald-trump-kkk-david-duke.
[81] Sam Stein, "Donald Trump Declines Three Chances to Disavow David Duke," *HuffPost*, February 28, 2016, retrieved on November, 29,

2016, http://www.huffpost.com/entry/donald-trump-david-duke_n_56d31097e4b0871f60ebbd35.
[82] *Ibid.*
[83] Janell Ross, "Why No One Should be Surprised that Donald Trump Didn't Disavow the KKK," *Washington Post*, February 29, 2016, retrieved on November 29, 2019, http://www.washingtonpost.com/news/the-fix/wp/2016/02/29/why-no-one-should-be-surprised-that-donald-trump-didnt-disavow-the-kkk.
[84] Timm.
[85] *Ibid*, et seq.
[86] Eugene Scott," Trump denounces David Duke, KKK," *CNN*, March 3, 2016, retrieved on November 29, 2019, http://www.cnn.com/2016/03/03/politics/donald-trump-disavows-david-duke-kkk/index.html.
[87] Katie Reilly, "Trump Says He Doesn't See White Nationalism as a Rising Global Threat after New Zealand Shooting," *Time*, March 15, 2019, retrieved on November 29, 2019, http://time.com/5552850/donald-trump-white-nationalism-global-threat-new-zealand.
[88] Chan.
[89] David A, Graham, "Five Things Trump Is Blaming for El Paso," *Atlantic*, August 5, 2019, retrieved on November 30, 2019, http://www.theatlantic.com/ideas/archive/2019/08/five-things-trump-blaming-el-paso/595492.
[90] Trump, "What I Saw at the Revolution," *New York Times*, February 19, 2000, retrieved on November 19, 2019, http://www.nytimes.com/2000/02/19/opinion/what-i-saw-at-the-revolution.html.
[91] Rebecca Hersher, "Jury Finds Dylann Roof Guilty in S.C. Church Shooting," *NPR*, December 15, 2016, retrieved on November 30, 2019, http://www.npr.org/sections/thetwo-way/2016/12/15/505723552/jury-finds-dylann-roof-guilty-in-s-c-church-shooting.
[92] *Ibid.*
[93] Alan Blinder and Kevin Sack, "Dylann Roof is Sentence to Death in Charleston Church Massacre," *New York Times*, January 10, 2017, retrieved on November 30, 2019, http://www.nytimes.com/2017/01/10/us/dylann-roof-trial-charleston.html.
[94] See, for example, Patrik Jonsson, "The Future of America's Past: should We 'explain' Confederate Statues?" *Christian Science Monitor*, August 22, 2019, retrieved on November 30, 2019, http://www.csmonitor.com/USA/Society/2019/0822/The-future-of-America-s-past-Should-we-explain-Confederate-statues.
[95] *Ibid.*

[96] Jonathan Zimmerman, "The Progressive Case for Keeping Confederate Statues Standing: We Shouldn't Cart away Reminders to Our White Supremacist History," *Daily News*, August 21, 2017, retrieved on November 30, 2019, http://www.nydailynews.com/opinion/progressive-case-keeping-confederate-statues-standing-article-1.3429164.
[97] *Ibid, et seq.*
[98] Jonsson.
[99] Josh Delk, "Trump on Tearing Down Confederate Statues: is George Washington Next?" *Hill*, August 15, 2017, retrieved on November 30, 2019, http://thehill.com/blogs/blog-briefing-room/346671-trump-on-tearing-down-of-confederate-statues-is-it-george-washington.
[100] Erin Blakemore, "The Largest Mass Deportation in American History," *History Channel*, March 23, 2018, retrieved on November 30, 2019, http://www.history.com/news/operation-wetback-eisenhower-1954-deportation.
[101] Tiffany Hsu, Kevin Draper, *et al.*, "In Plunge into Culture Wars, Nike Pulls an American Flag Sneaker," *New York Times*, B1, July 3, 2019.
[102] *Ibid.*
[103] Debbie Lord, "What Happened at Charlottesville: Looking back at the Rally That Ended in Death," *Atlanta Journal-Constitution*, August 10, 2018, retrieved on November 30, 2019, http://www.ajc.com/news/national/what-happened-charlottesville-looking-back-the-anniversary-the-deadly-rally/fPpnLrbAtbxSwNl9BEy93K.
[104] *Ibid, et seq.*
[105] Angie Drobnic Holan, "In Context: Trump's 'Very Fine People on Both Sides' Remarks (Transcript)," *PolitiFact*, April 26, 2019, retrieved on November 30, 2019, http://www.politifact.com/truth-o-meter/article/2019/apr/26/context-trumps-very-fine-people-both-sides-remarks.
[106] *Ibid, et seq.*
[107] Rosie Gray, "Trump Defends White-Nationalist Protesters: 'Some Very Fine People on Both Sides,'" *Atlantic*, August 15, 2017, retrieved on November 30, 2019, http://www.theatlantic.com/politics/archive/2017/08/trump-defends-white-nationalist-protesters-some-very-fine-people-on-both-sides/537012.
[108] Meghan Keneally, "Trump Lashes out at 'Alt-Left' in Charlottesville, Says 'Fine People on Both Sides'" *ABC News*, August 15, 2017, retrieved on November 30, 2019, http://abcnews.go.com/Politics/trump-lashes-alt-left-charlottesville-fine-people-sides/story?id=49235032.
[109] See, for example, Allan Smith, "Conway: Trump's Charlottesville Remarks 'Darn Near Perfection,'"

NBC News, April 28, 2019, retrieved on November 30, 2019, http://www.nbcnews.com/politics/donald-trump/conway-defends-trump-s-charlottesville-remarks-darn-near-perfection-n999266.
[110] Bess Levin, "Guy Who Dubbed Neo-Nazis 'Very Fine People' Suddenly Concerned about Anti-Semitism," *Vanity Fair*, March 6, 2019, retrieved on November 30, 2019, http://www.vanityfair.com/news/2019/03/donald-trump-ilhan-omar-democrats.
[111] *Ibid*.
[112] Will Sommer, "Trump Supporters Now Claim He Didn't Call Charlottesville Neo-Nazis 'Very Fine People," *Daily Beast*, April, 11, 2019, retrieved on December 1, 2019, http://www.thedailybeast.com/the-surprising-push-to-rebrand-trumps-very-fine-people-remarks.
[113] *Ibid*.
[114] NY Penal L § 130.05 (2019).
[115] *Ibid, et seq.*
[116] NJ Rev Stat § 2C:14-2 (2013)
[117] "Final Report Relating to Title 2C – Sexual Offenses," *New Jersey Law Revision Commission*, December 8, 2014.
[118] Fla. Stat. § 794 (2019). The offense is Sexual Battery; Matthew Choi, "Trump, a symbol of New York, is officially a Floridian now," *Politico*, October 31, 2019, retrieved on December 8, 2019, http://www.politico.com/states/florida/story/2019/10/31/trump-a-symbol-of-new-york-is-officially-a-floridian-now-1816915.
[119] David A. Fahrenthold, "Trump Recorded Having Extremely Lewd Conversation about Women in 2005," *Washington Post*, October 8, 2016, retrieved on December 8, 2019, http://www.washingtonpost.com/politics/trump-recorded-having-extremely-lewd-conversation-about-women-in-2005/2016/10/07/3b9ce776-8cb4-11e6-bf8a-3d26847eeed4_story.html.
[120] *Ibid, et seq.*
[121] Emily Arrowood, "They Very Definition of Sexual Assault," October 7, 2016, retrieved on December 14, 2019, http://www.usnews.com/opinion/articles/2016-10-07/hot-mic-catches-donald-trump-bragging-about-sexual-assault
[122] *Ibid*.
[123] Arthur Delaney, "Donald Trump Brushes off Sexual Assault Brag As 'Locker Room Talk,'" *HuffPost*, October 9, 2016, retrieved on December 8, 2019, http://www.huffpost.com/entry/trump-locker-room_n_57faeb1fe4b0b6a430334198.
[124] *Ibid, et seq.*
[125] Steven Benen, "Trump Haunted by His Record during Sexual Assault Prevention Month," *MSNBC*, April 3, 2017, retrieved on

December 8, 2019, http://www.msnbc.com/rachel-maddow-show/trump-haunted-his-record-during-sexual-assault-prevention-month.
[126] Ibid.
[127] Jill Filipovic, "The Awful Link Between Donald Trump's Rise and Bill Cosby's Sentence," *Vanity Fair*, September 25, 2018, retrieved on December 8, 2019, http://www.vanityfair.com/style/2018/09/bill-cosby-donald-trump-connection.
[128] Ibid, et seq.
[129] Mark Z. Barabak, "Donald Trump Has a Default Setting: What I Did May Be Bad, but Bill Clinton Has Done Even Worse," *Los Angeles Times*, October 7, 2016, retrieved on December 14, 2019, http://www.latimes.com/politics/la-na-pol-trump-bill-clinton-20161008-snap-story.html.
[130] Carlos Lozada, "How the Republican Party's Capitulation Gave us Donald Trump," *Washington Post*, July 18, 2019, retrieved on January 3, 2020, http://www.washingtonpost.com/outlook/2019/07/18/how-republican-partys-capitulation-gave-us-donald-trump.
[131] "Presidential Candidate Donald Trump Rally in Mount Pleasant, South Carolina," C-SPAN, December 7, 2015, retrieved on December 14, 2019, http://www.c-span.org/video/?401762-1/presidential-candidate-donald-trump-rally-mount-pleasant-south-carolina&start=1830.
[132] Ibid.
[133] See, for example, Lauren Carroll and Louis Jacobson, "Trump Cites Shaky Survey in Call to Ban Muslims from Entering U.S.," *PolitiFact*, December 9, 2015, retrieved on December 14, 2019, http://www.politifact.com/truth-o-meter/statements/2015/dec/09/donald-trump/trump-cites-shaky-survey-call-ban-muslims-entering.
[134] Ibid.
[135] Gul Tuysuz, "What is Sharia Law?" *CNN*, August 16, 2016, retrieved on December 14, 2019, http://www.cnn.com/2016/08/16/world/sharia-law-definition/index.html.
[136] Kyle Blaine and Julia Horowitz, "How the Trump Administration Chose the 7 Countries in the Immigration Executive Order," *CNN*, January 30, 2017, retrieved on December 15, 2019, http://www.cnn.com/2017/01/29/politics/how-the-trump-administration-chose-the-7-countries/index.html.
[137] Ibid.
[138] Trump, "Executive Order 13679, Protecting the Nation From Foreign Terrorist Entry Into the United States," Federal Register, January 27, 2017, retrieved on December 15, 2019, http://www.federalregister.gov/documents/2017/02/01/2017-02281/protecting-the-nation-from-foreign-terrorist-entry-into-the-united-states.

[139] *Ibid*, et seq.

[140] Editorial, "Donald Trump's Muslim Ban is Cowardly and Dangerous," *New York Times*, January 28, 2017, retrieved on http://www.nytimes.com/2017/01/28/opinion/donald-trumps-muslim-ban-is-cowardly-and-dangerous.html.

[141] Benen, "Trump's Muslim ban Causes Turmoil within the Administration," *MSNBC*, January 31, 2017, retrieved on December 16, 2019, http://www.msnbc.com/rachel-maddow-show/trumps-muslim-ban-causes-turmoil-within-the-administration.

[142] Chris Sommerfeldt, "President Trump's Muslim Ban Excludes Countries Linked to His Sprawling Business Empire," *Daily News*, February 1, 2017, retrieved on December 16, 2019, http://www.nydailynews.com/news/politics/trump-muslim-ban-excludes-countries-linked-businesses-article-1.2957956.

[143] Rebecca Shabad, "Trump's New Travel Ban Executive Order Removes Iraq from List of Banned Countries," *CBS News*, March 6, 2017, retrieved on December 19, 2019, http://www.cbsnews.com/news/trumps-new-travel-ban-executive-order.

[144] Trump, "Presidential Proclamation Enhancing Vetting Capabilities and Processes for Detecting Attempted Entry Into the United States by Terrorists or Other Public-Safety Threats," White House, September 24, 2017, retrieved on December 19, 2019, http://www.whitehouse.gov/presidential-actions/presidential-proclamation-enhancing-vetting-capabilities-processes-detecting-attempted-entry-united-states-terrorists-public-safety-threats.

[145] *Trump v. Hawaii*, 138 S. Ct. 2392 (2018); Hilary Hurd and Yishai Schwartz, "The Supreme Court Travel Ban Ruling: a Summary," *Lawfare*, June 26, 2018, retrieved on December 20, 2019, http://www.lawfareblog.com/supreme-court-travel-ban-ruling-summary.

[146] See, examples, Jay Michaelson, "Trump's Muslim Ban is Destroying These Americans' Lives, Two Years On," *Daily Beast*, January 28, 2019, retrieved on December 19, 2019, http://www.thedailybeast.com/trumps-muslim-ban-is-destroying-these-americans-lives-two-years-on; Rowaida Abdelaziz, "2 Years Later, Trump's Muslim Ban is Still Keeping Families Apart," February 2, 2019, retrieved on December 19, 2019, http://www.huffpost.com/entry/trump-muslim-ban-2-years_n_5c50b9dae4b00906b26e2ee4; Farida Chehata, "The Continuing Cost of the Trump Muslim Ban," *Daily News*, May 13, 2019, retrieved on December 19, 2019, http://www.dailynews.com/2019/05/13/the-continuing-cost-of-the-trump-muslim-ban.

[147] Jeff Diamant, "The Countries with the 10 largest Christian Populations and the 10 largest Muslim Populations, *Pew Research Center*, April 1 2019, retrieved on December 20, 2019, http://www.pewresearch.org/fact-tank/2019/04/01/the-countries-with-

the-10-largest-christian-populations-and-the-10-largest-muslim-populations.
[148] *Ibid, et seq.*
[149] U.S. Department of State statistics for 2018 for immigrant and nonimmigrant visas issued, retrieved on December 20, 2019, (immigrant visas) http://travel.state.gov/content/dam/visas/Statistics/AnnualReports/FY2018AnnualReport/FY18AnnualReport%20-%20TableIII.pdf; (nonimmigrant visas) https://travel.state.gov/content/dam/visas/Statistics/AnnualReports/FY2018AnnualReport/FY18AnnualReport%20-%20TableXVIII.pdf.
[150] *Ibid.*
[151] "Global Religious Futures Project (2020 Projections)" *Pew Research Center,* retrieved on December 20, 2019, http://www.globalreligiousfutures.org/countries/china#/?affiliations_religion_id=0&affiliations_year=2020&region_name=All%20Countries&restrictions_year=2016.
[152] M.K. Holder, "Why are More People Right-Handed?" *Scientific American*, November 1, 2001, retrieved December 20, 2019, http://www.scientificamerican.com/article/why-are-more-people-right.
[153] Doyle Rice, "Dorian's Legacy: the Slowest, Strongest Hurricane to Ever Hit the Bahamas," *USA Today*, September 6, 2019, retrieved on December 24, 2019, http://www.usatoday.com/story/news/nation/2019/09/06/hurricane-dorian-becomes-strongest-slowest-hurricane-hit-bahamas-record/2232225001.
[154] Rachel Frazin and Tal Axelrod, "Death and Destruction: a Timeline of Hurricane Dorian," *The Hill*, September 6, 2019, retrieved on December 26, 2019, http://thehill.com/homenews/news/460373-death-and-destruction-a-timeline-of-hurricane-dorian.
[155] Trump, *Twitter*, September 1, 2019, retrieved on December 26, 2019, http://twitter.com/realDonaldTrump/status/1168174613827899393?ref_src=twsrc%5Egoogle%7Ctwcamp%5Eserp%7Ctwgr%5Etweet.
[156] Kenneth T. Walsh, "The Undoing of George W. Bush," *U.S. News & World Report*, August 28, 2015, retrieved on December 26, 2019, https://www.usnews.com/news/the-report/articles/2015/08/28/hurricane-katrina-was-the-beginning-of-the-end-for-george-w-bush.
[157] *Ibid.*
[158] *Ibid*; Joe Johns, "Sen. Lott's Home Destroyed by Katrina," *CNN*, September 4, 2005, retrieved on December 26, 2019, http://www.cnn.com/2005/POLITICS/08/30/katrina.lott.
[159] Walsh.

[160] Douglas Brinkley, "The Flood that Sank George W. Bush," *Vanity Fair*, August 26, 2015, retrieved on December 26, 2019, http://www.vanityfair.com/news/2015/08/hurricane-katrina-george-w-bush-new-orleans.
[161] Brian Stelter, "Trump Claimed Dorian Could Hit Alabama -- Even after Weather Service Refuted it," *CNN*, September 3, 2019, retrieved on December 26, 2019, http://www.cnn.com/2019/09/02/politics/trump-hurricane-dorian-false-claims-alabama/index.html.
[162] *Ibid.*
[163] Trevor Nace, "Alabama's NWS Had a Perfect Response to Trump's Dorian Tweet," *Forbes*, September 2, 2019, retrieved on December 26, 2019, http://www.forbes.com/sites/trevornace/2019/09/02/alabamas-nws-had-a-perfect-response-to-trumps-dorian-tweet/#38cc491d26a7.
[164] Smith, "Why Does Trump's Hurricane Map Look Different from Others?" *NBC News*, September 4, 2019, retrieved on December 26, 2019, http://www.nbcnews.com/politics/donald-trump/why-does-trumps-hurricane-map-look-different-others-n1049711.
[165] David K. Li, The Sharpie is Mightier: Trump Mocked after That Map of Dorian's Path," *NBC News*, September 5, 2019, retrieved on December 26, 2019, http://www.nbcnews.com/politics/donald-trump/sharpie-mightier-trump-mocked-after-map-dorian-s-path-n1049966.
[166] Toluse Olorunnipa and Josh Dawsey, "'What I said was accurate!': Trump Stays Fixated on his Alabama Error as Hurricane Pounds the Carolinas," *Washington Post*, September 5, 2019, retrieved on December 26, 2019, http://www.washingtonpost.com/politics/what-i-said-was-accurate-trump-stays-fixated-on-his-alabama-error-as-hurricane-pounds-the-carolinas/2019/09/05/32597606-cfe7-11e9-8c1c-7c8ee785b855_story.html.
[167] *Ibid, et seq.*
[168] Alabama Electoral History, *270 to Win,* retrieved on December 26, 2016, http://www.270towin.com/states/Alabama.
[169] Richard Gonzalez, "NOAA Contradicts Weather Service, Backs Trump on Hurricane Threat in Alabama," *NPR*, September 6, 2019, retrieved on December 26, 2019, http://www.npr.org/2019/09/06/758532041/noaa-contradicts-weather-service-backs-trump-on-hurricane-threat-in-alabama.
[170] *Ibid, et seq.*
[171] Tara Law and Gina Martinez, "NOAA Disputes Its Own Experts, Siding with President Trump over Hurricane Dorian and Alabama. Here's a Full Timeline of the Controversy," *Time*, September 8, 2019, retrieved on December 26, 2019, http://time.com/5671606/trump-hurricane-dorian-alabama.
[172] See, for example, Liz Spikol, "I May Live in Pennsylvania, but I'm no Pennsylvanian," *Philadelphia*, January 31, 2016, retrieved on

December 27, 2019, http://www.phillymag.com/news/2016/01/31/pennsylvania-pennsyltucky-philadelphia; Ben Smith, "Obama on Small-town Pa.: Clinging to Religion, Guns, Xenophobia," April 11, 2008, retrieved on December 27, 2019, http://www.politico.com/blogs/ben-smith/2008/04/obama-on-small-town-pa-clinging-to-religion-guns-xenophobia-007737.

[173] Carrie Budoff Brown, "Extreme Makeover: Pennsylvania Edition," *Politico*, April 1, 2008, retrieved on December 27, 2019, http://www.politico.com/story/2008/04/extreme-makeover-pennsylvania-edition-009323.

[174] *Ibid*.

[175] Scaros, "What a Trump Rally is Really Like" *The National Herald*, April 30, 2016, 1.

[176] *Ibid*.

[177] Ashleigh Banfield, "Mashup of Trump Praising Violence against Protesters," *CNN*, March 12, 2016, retrieved on December 27, 2019, http://www.cnn.com/videos/politics/2016/03/12/donald-trump-rallies-violence-protests-mashup-lv.cnn.

[178] *Ibid, et seq*.

[179] Aianara Tiefenhaler, "Trump's History of Encouraging Violence," *New York Times*, March 14, 2016, retrieved on December 28, 2019, http://www.nytimes.com/video/us/100000004269364/trump-and-violence.html.

[180] Harry S. Truman, Letter to Paul Hume, Truman Library, December 6, 1950, retrieved on December 28, 2019, http://www.trumanlibrary.gov/education/trivia/letter-truman-defends-daughter-singing.

[181] Rachel Gillett and Allana Akhtar, "These are the top 20 US Presidents (and Why You Won't Find Trump on the List)," *Business Insider*, July 4, 2019, retrieved on December 28, 2019, http://www.businessinsider.com/the-top-20-presidents-in-us-history-according-to-historians-2017-2.

[182] *Ibid, et seq*.

[183] Noah Berlatsky, "Is Trump a Fascist? Learning about How Fascism Works Can Help Prevent its Spread in America," *NBC News*, September 3, 2018, retrieved on December 30, 2019, http://www.nbcnews.com/think/opinion/trump-fascist-learning-about-how-fascism-works-can-help-prevent-ncna905886.

[184] *Ibid, et seq*.

[185] Jacqueline Thomsen, "Madeleine Albright: Trump is the Most anti-Democratic President in American History, *The Hill*, April 4, 2018, retrieved on December 30, 2019, http://thehill.com/homenews/administration/381552-madeleine-albright-trump-is-the-most-anti-democratic-president-in.

[186] *Ibid, et seq.*
[187] Jonathan Chait, "Trump and the Rhetoric of Fascism," *New York*, June 20, 2019, retrieved on December 30, 2019, http://nymag.com/intelligencer/2019/06/trump-and-the-rhetoric-of-fascism.html.
[188] *Ibid, et seq.*
[189] Editors, "President John Adams Oversees Passage of first of Alien and Sedition Acts," *History Channel*, July 28, 2019, retrieved on December 30, 2019, http://www.history.com/this-day-in-history/adams-passes-first-of-alien-and-sedition-acts.
[190] *Ibid, et seq.*
[191] Editors, "U.S. Congress Passes Sedition Act," *History Channel,* July 28, 2019, retrieved on December 30, 2019, http://www.history.com/this-day-in-history/u-s-congress-passes-sedition-act.
[192] Marc Jacob, "Trump, Biden, and 5 Other Pols Who Talked about Punching People," *Chicago Tribune*, March 22, 2018, retrieved on December 30, 2019, http://www.chicagotribune.com/news/ct-met-trump-biden-punching-5-things-20180322-story.html.
[193] Ryan Browne, "Why Did the U.S. Bomb Hiroshima?" *CNN*, May 27, 2016, retrieved on December 30, 2019, http://www.cnn.com/2016/05/27/politics/hiroshima-obama-explainer/index.html.
[194] *Ibid, et seq.*
[195] Gillett.
[196] U.S. Congress, House, H.R. 347, January 3, 2012.
[197] *The Sopranos*(1999-2007), *Boardwalk Empire* 2009-2014), and *On the Waterfront* (1954) were two television series and a film, respectively, with plots involving violent intimidation to suppress or promote particular views and behavior.
[198] Madeleine Sheehan Perkins, "A Complete Timeline of Trump's Years-Long Feud with Rosie O' Donnell," *Business Insider*, May 12, 2017, retrieved on December 30, 2019, http://www.businessinsider.com/trump-rosie-odonnell-history-2017-5.
[199] Trump, Twitter, July 14, 2019, retrieved on December 31, 2019, http://twitter.com/realDonaldTrump/status/1150381394234941448?ref_src=twsrc%5Etfw%7Ctwcamp%5Etweetembed%7Ctwterm%5E1150443496345624577&ref_url=https%.
[200] Kate Sullivan, "Here are the 4 Congresswomen Known as 'The Squad' Targeted by Trump's Racist Tweets," *CNN*, July 16, 2019, retrieved on December 31, 2019, http://www.cnn.com/2019/07/15/politics/who-are-the-squad/index.html.
[201] See, for example, Sanjana Karanth, "Federal Law Says 'Go Back to Where You Came from' Counts as Discrimination," *HuffPost*, July 17, 2019, retrieved on January 1, 2020,

http://www.huffpost.com/entry/federal-law-go-back-came-from-discrimination_n_5d2e815de4b085eda5a390cc.

[202] Sintia Radu, "Records that Countries Broke in 2019," *U.S. News & World Report*, December 27, 2019, retrieved on January 1, 2020, http://www.usnews.com/news/best-countries/slideshows/these-are-the-records-that-countries-broke-in-2019.

[203] Congress, Biographical Directory, retrieved on January 1, 2020, http://bioguide.congress.gov/biosearch/biosearch.asp.

[204] Margaret Hoover, "The Firing Line," PBS, July 13, 2018, retrieved on January 1, 2019, http://www.pbs.org/video/alexandria-ocasio-cortez-barhhq/

[205] *Ibid*.

[206] Brett Samuels, "Trump Shares Graham Quote Calling Ocasio-Cortez 'anti-America,'" *The Hill*, July 15, 2019, retrieved on January 1, 2020, http://thehill.com/homenews/administration/453062-trump-shares-graham-quote-calling-ocasio-cortez-anti-america.

[207] Cody Nelson, "Minnesota Congresswoman Ignites Debate on Israel and Anti-Semitism," *NPR*, March 7, 2019, retrieved on January 1, 2020, http://www.npr.org/2019/03/07/700901834/minnesota-congresswoman-ignites-debate-on-israel-and-anti-semitism.

[208] Rebecca Klar, "Pressley: Democrats Don't need 'Any More Black Faces that Don't Want to be a Black Voice," *The Hill*, July 14, 2019, retrieved on January 1, 2020, http://thehill.com/homenews/house/453007-pressley-democrats-need-any-more-black-voices-that-dont-want-to-be-a-black.

[209] Kelsey Snell, Pelosi Clashes with Progressive 'Squad' as Internal Party Tensions Get Personal," *NPR*, July 11, 2019, retrieved on January 1, 2020, http://www.npr.org/2019/07/11/740721823/pelosi-clashes-with-progressive-squad-as-internal-party-tensions-get-personal.

[210] Dwyer, "'Go Back Where You Came from': the Long Rhetorical Roots of Trump's Racist Tweets," *NPR*, July 15, 2019, retrieved on January 1, 2020, http://www.npr.org/2019/07/15/741827580/go-back-where-you-came-from-the-long-rhetorical-roots-of-trump-s-racist-tweets.

[211] *Ibid*.

[212] Lissandra Villa and Charlotte Alter, "The Second Democratic Debates Could Be all about Trump's Racist Tweets," *Time*, July 29, 2019, retrieved on January 1, 2020, http://time.com/5638265/second-democratic-debates-trump-racist-tweets.

[213] John Haltiwanger, "Timeline of the Chaotic Series of events Surrounding Trump's Racist Tweets Attacking 'the Squad,'" July 20, 2019, retrieved on January 1, 2020, http://www.businessinsider.com/timeline-of-events-surrounding-trumps-racist-tweets-at-the-squad-2019-7.

[214] Bianca Quilantan and David Cohen, "Trump Tells Dem Congresswomen: Go Back Where You Came from," July 14, 2019, retrieved on January 1, 2020, http://www.politico.com/story/2019/07/14/trump-congress-go-back-where-they-came-from-1415692.
[215] Devan Cole, "Trump Tweets Racist Attacks at Progressive Democratic Congresswomen," *CNN*, July 14, 2019, retrieved on January 1, 2020, http://www.cnn.com/2019/07/14/politics/donald-trump-tweets-democratic-congresswomen-race-nationalities/index.html.
[216] Alistair Bell, "The Long Road to Trump's Impeachment and Trial," *Reuters*, February 5, 2020, retrieved on February 8, 2020, http://www.reuters.com/article/us-usa-trump-impeachment-timeline/the-long-road-to-trumps-impeachment-and-trial-idUSKBN1ZZ2EI.
[217] Ron Johnson, Letter, November 18, 2019, retrieved on February 8, 2020, http://www.ronjohnson.senate.gov/public/_cache/files/e0b73c19-9370-42e6-88b1-b2458eaeeecd/johnson-to-jordan-nunes.pdf.
[218] *Ibid, et seq.*
[219] Bell.
[220] Ron Johnson.
[221] See, for example, Philip Ewing, "The Trump-Ukraine Affair: What You Need to Know and What's Coming Next, *NPR,* September 27, 2019, retrieved on February 8, 2020, http://www.npr.org/2019/09/27/764794409/the-trump-ukraine-affair-what-you-need-to-know-and-whats-coming-next; Jonathan Allen, "Witnesses Take a Toll on Trump's Impeachment Defenses," *NBC News*, November 19, 2019, retrieved on February 8, 2020, http://www.nbcnews.com/politics/trump-impeachment-inquiry/very-bad-impeachment-hearings-day-donald-trump-n1086441; and Zachary Wolf and Sean O'Key, "The Trump-Ukraine Impeachment Inquiry Report, Annotated," *CNN*, December 3, 2019, retrieved on February 8, 2020, http://www.cnn.com/interactive/2019/12/politics/trump-ukraine-impeachment-inquiry-report-annotated.
[222] Johnson; "Memorandum of [Trump-Zelensky] Telephone Conversation [of July 25 2019]," White House, September 24, 2019, retrieved on February 8, 2020, http://www.whitehouse.gov/wp-content/uploads/2019/09/Unclassified09.2019.pdf.
[223] Johnson.
[224] Ewing, "'Not Guilty': Trump Acquitted on 2 Articles of Impeachment as Historic Trial Closes," *NPR*, February 5, 2020, retrieved on February 8, 2020, http://www.npr.org/2020/02/05/801429948/not-guilty-trump-acquitted-on-2-articles-of-impeachment-as-historic-trial-closes.

Made in the USA
Middletown, DE
17 May 2020